D0762631

Enactments

EDITED BY RICHARD SCHECHNER

To perform is to imagine, represent, live and enact present
circumstances, past events and future possibilities. Performance takes place
across a very broad range of venues from city streets to the countryside, in
theatres and in offices, on battlefields and in hospital operating rooms. The
genres of performance are many, from the arts to the myriad performances of
everyday life, from courtrooms to
legislative chambers, from theatres to wars to circuses.

ENACTMENTS will encompass performance in as many of its aspects and
realities as there are authors able to write about them.

ENACTMENTS will include active scholarship, readable thought and engaged
analysis across the broad spectrum of
performance studies.

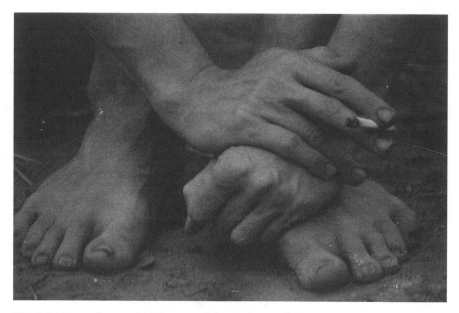

FIGURE 1: Jerzy Grotowski. Photograph by Andrzej Paluchiewicz.

GROTOWSKI'S BRIDGE MADE OF MEMORY

Embodied Memory, Witnessing and Transmission in the Grotowski Work

DOMINIKA LASTER

CALCUTTA LONDON NEW YORK

Jurkowi
To those who came before
Iliaszkowi
and those who come after.

Seagull Books, 2016

© Dominika Laster, 2016

All photographs © Individual photographers and/or owners

ISBN 978 0 8574 2 317 7

British Library Cataloguing-in-Publication Data
A catalogue record for this book is available from the British Library

Typeset by Seagull Books, Calcutta, India
Printed and bound by Hyam Enterprises, Calcutta, India

FIGURE 2: Jerzy Grotowski. Photograph by Andrzej Paluchiewicz.

To cross the boundaries with your whole being,
with honesty, discipline, and precision.
This is the method, nothing else.

Jerzy Grotowski

CONTENTS

Acknowledgements   *ix*

Preface   *xii*

INTRODUCTION   1

CHAPTER 1
EMBODIED MEMORY
Grotowski's Work on Personal and Ancestral memories   21

CHAPTER 2
CZUWAJ (BE VIGILANT)
Vigilance and Witnessing in the Grotowski Work   57

CHAPTER 3
GROTOWSKI'S LADDER
Making the Archaic Vertical Connection   93

CHAPTER 4
'LET ME TAKE YOU TO THE LAND OF YOUR ANCESTORS'
Grotowski and Transmission   121

Epilogue   147

References   153

Index   160

ACKNOWLEDGEMENTS

I am deeply grateful to Richard Schechner for his incredible support of this project. I am forever indebted to him for pulling me into the adventure of Tracing Grotowski's Path: Year of Grotowski in New York, a six-month-long series of events coinciding with UNESCO's designation of 2009 as the 'Year of Grotowski' consisting of workshops, panel discussions, film screenings and a photograph exhibition that took place in a variety of New York venues including Lincoln Center, La MaMa Experimental Theatre Club, Tisch School of the Arts/NYU and the CUNY Graduate Center, among others. In many ways Tracing Grotowski's Path nurtured this manuscript. Professor Schechner's unyielding commitment, keen insights and proposed challenges have contributed greatly towards deepening this work.

I wish to thank Diana Taylor for awakening within me a profound interest in memory and witnessing. Professor Taylor's work and pedagogy have been a tremendous source of inspiration.

I thank Barbara Kirshenblatt-Gimblett, whose brilliant and imaginative mind never ceases to amaze me. I am very grateful to her for always showing me how to look at things in new and unexpected ways.

I would like to thank Professors Daniel Gerould and Michał Kobiałka, whose pioneering work on Polish theatre continues to be an endless source of inspiration.

I am deeply grateful to Sterling Professor Joseph Roach and the Mellon Fellowship in interdisciplinary performance studies at Yale University, which has given me the opportunity to deepen and extend my research. It has been a great privilege to work alongside such distinguished colleagues during my tenure at Yale University.

I gratefully acknowledge the Grotowski Institute for the financial support that allowed me to travel to Wrocław to attend the inauguration of the Year of Grotowski and to conduct research in the Grotowski archive. In particular, I wish to thank the institute's director, Jarosław Fret, as well as Bruno Chojak and Magdalena Mądra.

I am forever indebted to Joanna Klass for her kindness and help in the facilitation of my research.

I also wish to take this opportunity to thank Stefania Gardecka, who granted me—and scores of other broke teenagers—free access to the events at the Grotowski Centre. It was this opening that planted the seeds for my deep and lifelong interest in the work of Grotowski.

I wish to acknowledge the Polish Cultural Institute in New York for their initiative and partnership in the organization of the Year of Grotowski in New York events, of which I am grateful to have been a part. In particular, I thank Director Monika Fabijańska, Deputy Director Agata Grenda, as well as Chief Administrative Officer Piotr Rogulski and Graphic Designer Marcelina Knitter.

I owe special gratitude to Sara Brady whose keen eye and incisive editorial work has brought much clarity to this writing. I also wish to thank the team at Seagull Books for the elegance and precision of their editorial preparation of this manuscript.

This book would not have been possible had it not been for the knowledge, generosity and openness of the people who gave their time to talk to me.

I am especially grateful to Thomas Richards for the interview that constitutes the heart of Chapter 1. I thank him, Cécile Berthe, and Eliot Richards for opening their home to me.

I wish to thank Mario Biagini for his warmth, generosity and guidance. Our conversations contributed greatly to my understanding of the themes with which I engage in this book.

I am very grateful to Andrzej Paluchiewicz for permission to use his photographs. I thank him and Lidia Majerczak for allowing me to stay in their home while conducting research at the Grotowski Institute in Wrocław.

I am grateful to Mieczysław Janowski for his incredible enthusiasm, warmth and openness and for the experience of 'translating him' into English.

In addition, I wish to thank: Ludwik Flaszen, Rena Mirecka and Maud Robart. I am very grateful to the people who have enriched this book through their interviews with me: Marianne Ahrne, Jairo Cuesta, Katharina Seyferth and Professor Zbigniew Osiński.

I am very grateful to Kermit Dunkelberg and Sebastian Rypson for their generosity in sharing their work with me and for our email discussions about Grotowski and Haiti.

My email correspondence with Marina Gregory, Julia Ulehla and Tim Hopfner of the Workcenter of Jerzy Grotowski and Thomas Richards helped me get through the last phases of this writing. I thank them for their warmth, humour, and encouragement.

I also wish to thank Krzysztof Bednarski and Marek Musiał for permission to use their photographs in this publication. I thank him and Lidia Majerczak for allowing me to stay in their home while conducting research at the Grotowski institute in Wrocław.

Thank you to Magda Złotowska—for being.

I am very thankful to my friends, Heidi Kling, Michelle Lindenblatt, Angela Marino, Megan Nicely, Dana Okrinova, Beata Potocki, Aniko Szucs and Monika Weryho for their encouragement and support.

Finally, I wish to thank my parents Stefania and Jakub Laster for their love and support. I am also very grateful to Elżbieta Laster, for the gift on which this book was written.

It was nearly midnight one winter when I finished mending the holes of an old Polish army backpack that my friend presented to me upon hearing of my impending journey. Early next morning I would take a bus to the outskirts of Wrocław, Poland, and begin my three-day hitchhiking journey through the Alps. My destination—The Workcenter of Jerzy Grotowski, Pontedera, Italy.

The year was 1995 and I was a second-year student of theatre theory at the Jagiellonian University in Kraków. Initially, I had planned to take the polite route—to finish my studies and somehow miraculously enter Grotowski's work circle. It's not that I was unhappy living in a city haunted by the ghosts of Tadeusz Kantor's *Dead Class*. Nonetheless, I had come to the realization that I was leading a life of half-measures, putting off what I really wanted to do simply because I was afraid. I feared not only the possibility of not being accepted into the Workcenter but, perhaps more poignantly, of being disillusioned. What had once been a strong desire to work with Grotowski had now been relegated to the role of a distant dream, a pleasant story I told my friends and myself about. This self-revelation was a turning point that catalyzed a series of actions and the journey I now relate.

Having arrived at this new understanding of myself, I went to the Centre for Study of Jerzy Grotowski[1] and asked Pani Stefa[2] for the address of Grotowski's Workcenter in Italy. At the time, the exact location of the Workcenter was still not widely known, and seemed to be shrouded in secrecy. Afraid to ask too many questions for fear that someone might surmise my covert plan, I did not find out that Grotowski conducted periodic selections sessions at his Workcenter. I decided against writing to him in advance, for fear of being told not to come. Anyway, I reasoned, my presence at his doorstep would be stronger than any argument I could convey by letter.

The three days that it took me to carry out my quest through the February Alps proved nothing compared to the emotional leap I had to take to arrive in Pontedera. Being an extremist, I burnt all my bridges. I did not cautiously take a leave of absence from the university. I did not sublet my apartment. I liquidated everything and left without giving myself the option of being able to return to Poland.

I travelled with less than 20 dollars in my pocket. A truck dropped me off on the outskirts of Pontedera and I searched for via Indipendenza. It was past 11 at night when I finally found the address I had exacted. I saw lights in the windows of the second floor and heard noise coming from inside. I knocked, but got no response. I decided to wait. Sure enough, about half an hour later, a group of people began to pour out onto the street. 'Is this the Workcenter of Jerzy Grotowski?' I asked the first person to exit. It turned out that what I had found was actually the Centro per la Sperimentazione e la Ricerca Teatrale,[3] a host institution for the Workcenter, the address of which Grotowski used for correspondence. 'Well, could you tell me the location of the Workcenter?' I pursued. 'Oh, it is very difficult to find. You must go through forests, cross mountains and rivers. It is unlikely that you will ever find it without a guide,' the man answered. 'Have you been there?' I probed. 'Yes, but it was long ago.' It was clear that he would not tell me. 'Could you point me in the general direction?' He gestured east. I thanked him and started walking.

FIGURE 3: Wrocław, Rynek-Ratusz 27 during the University of Research (1975). Photograph by Andrzej Paluchiewicz.

I kept walking, leaving the city behind me. Once out of the reach of city lights, I realized that I could not see more than a few feet in front of me and that continuing on this moonless night would be futile. I decided to spend the night in Pontedera and reassess my strategy. In the morning, I went again to the theatre. This time my questioning resulted in a crucial piece of information, which my informant 'accidentally' let slip: the Workcenter is near the village of La Rotta. I was on the next bus to La Rotta.

Once there, I walked into the only—from what I could see—public locale in the village, and everyone froze. Everyone turned to look at the *estranea*. 'Dove è il Centro di Lavoro di Jerzy Grotowski?' I stammered in my broken Italian, which I had learnt from the drivers who picked me up south of the border. Silence. 'Teatro sperimentale,' I ventured. 'Ah, il professore!' Someone told me to go straight, over the railroad tracks, and then turn right. Somehow, I understood. I followed the directions, and after a 10-minute walk, reached some edifices. I walked up to the first building, which looked to me like an old barn, climbed the stairs and knocked. A man opened. I had interrupted him. I stated again my query, this time in English. This man, who I would later learn was Thomas Richards,[4] pointed to a man walking down a path in our direction: 'Talk to him.'

The second man was tall with dirty-blonde hair. 'Is this the Workcenter of Jerzy Grotowski? Is Jerzy Grotowski here?' I asked him. 'Maybe he is, maybe he isn't. Either way, you are not going to see him.' This was my first encounter with Mario Biagini.[5] In the course of the conversation that ensued, I learnt that Grotowski was in a hospital in France. Knowing that no one but Grotowski could grant me permission to stay, I asked Mario for advice. He told me to write Grotowski a letter and wait for a response. 'But I have no return address,' I told him. 'Well, then get one.'

How I finally did meet Grotowski would require the telling of another story. However, when I found myself sitting across from him and listening to him speak as he tore off the filter of yet another Camel Extra Strong, I was satisfied that he not only confirmed but surpassed all that I had previously intuited about the man and his work.

I first became conscious of Grotowski's work at the age of 16, when I came across a tattered photocopy of the Laboratory Theatre's internal document entitled

'Statement of Principles'. However, I had been exposed to 'Grotowski' much earlier and in a manner that was much more indirect. My mother's friendship
with Laboratory Theatre actors—Ryszard Cieślak, Andrzej Paluchiewicz and
Mieczysław Janowski, among others—created a proximity to the theatre culture
nascent in Wrocław at that time. Later, as a student of Autorska Szkoła Samorozwoju (literally: Authors' School for Self-Development),[6] an experimental high
school in Wrocław, I spent all of my free time at the Grotowski Centre attending
lectures, talks and film screenings, and participating in workshops with Laboratory Theatre actors including Zygmunt Molik, as well as other Grotowski collaborators such as Maud Robart.

The Grotowski Centre, situated in the very heart of the old town, inherited
the address Wrocław, Rynek-Ratusz 27—a point of destination for many—
along with the buildings that formerly housed the Laboratory Theatre. After
the Laboratory Theatre's official dissolution in 1984, the buildings were home
to the Second Studio (Drugie Studio Wrocławskie), whose goal was to train a
new ensemble of actors while at the same time take over the care and mainte-
nance of archival materials and the physical remnants of the Laboratory. The
Second Studio was led by one of the principal actors of the Laboratory Theatre,
Zbigniew Cynkutis. After Cynkutis' tragic death in January of 1987, Mirosław
Kocur became the artistic director of the Second Studio until its dissolution in
1989. Subsequently, Zbigniew Osiński founded the Grotowski Centre, whose
opening roughly coincided with the fall of communism.

For me as well as many of my friends and colleagues the Grotowski Centre
constituted the heart of the cultural and artistic life in Wrocław in the 1990s.
Its programming and mode of operation drew explicitly on some of the tenets
of Grotowski's work. Looking back at the first decade of the Centre's operation,
Osiński retrospectively states that his objectives for the Centre included: to
establish a space not governed by the domain of official or dominant culture;
to promulgate values that fall outside of the purview of the establishment; and
to build bridges between the arts and sciences, between the past and the present
with an eye to the future (2001b: 3). Moreover, speaking more generally about
alternative cultural centres that surfaced in Poland around the brink of the fall
of communism, Osiński states:

Complementarity vis-à-vis dominant culture, dialogicality, openness,
activity which is 'in-between', merging theory with practice, creating

a form of communication between people which is different than that of official culture; one which is more integral, comprehensive, appeals to the totality of the human being, is free of coquetry and independent of the official and social hierarchies—these are the fundamental features of [Polish cultural] centres of the 1990s (ibid.: 7).[7]

While today I am sceptical about the possibility of a cultural institution approaching the goals outlined above without falling into the very traps it aims to evade, as a person coming of age in Wrocław in the 1990s, for me the institutional activity of the Grotowski Centre seemed to model the very tenets of Grotowski's work which it sought to embody. Admittedly, this activity must have been a mere flicker of the intensity of the cultural activity of Wrocław in the 1970s and early 1980s.

Beyond the Laboratory Theatre productions and paratheatrical activity, I have in mind such large-scale events as the University of Research. Organized under the framework of the Theatre of Nations (1975), the University of Research featured events such as seminars, workshops, performances, public meetings, films, demonstrations and Paratheatre events that included over 5,000 participants from 23 nations, among them such theatre luminaries as Eugenio Barba, Jean-Louis Barrault, Peter Brook, Joseph Chaikin, André Gregory and Luca Ronconi. However, the Grotowski Centre managed to keep alive something of the previous life which the buildings of Wrocław, Rynek-Ratusz 27 held and let spill onto the streets. It was in the so-called Apocalypsis room of the Laboratory Theatre that I first heard Peter Brook discuss George Gurdjieff; worked on the body and voice with Zygmunt Molik; learnt Haitian traditional songs and ritual movement of the *yanvalou* from Maud Robart; witnessed Odin Teatret actor Roberta Carreri perform her one-woman show *Judith*; and saw an exhibition of Tadeusz Kantor's *emballages*. Reading Grzegorz Ziółkowski's[8] personal reminiscences about the Grotowski Centre, I realize that the quintessence of the meaning it held for me is shared by at least a handful of others of my generation for whom the activities of the Grotowski Centre provided not only an alternative or supplementary education but in fact constituted its core (2001: 60).

Notes

1 Ośrodek Badań Twórczości Jerzego Grotowskiego i Poszukiwań Teatralno-Kultur-owych (The Centre for Study of Jerzy Grotowski's Work and of the Cultural and Theatrical Research [*sic*]) started its activities in 1990 under the direction of Zbigniew Osiński in the Laboratory Theatre buildings. This institution, which changed its name in 2006 to the Grotowski Institute, is devoted to documenting and researching the artistic activities of Grotowski and the Laboratory Theatre, as well as organizing international meetings, conferences, and theatre workshops.

2 Stefania Gardecka, known to many as Pani (Ms) Stefa or simply Stefa, was Grotowski's long-term administrative assistant who worked in the Laboratory Theatre in Wrocław, Poland, from 1966 to 1984. From its inception, she worked at the Grotowski Centre in Wrocław and continued her collaboration with the Grotowski Institute until November 2009.

3 Today, the Fondazione Pontedera Teatro.

4 Thomas Richards began working systematically with Grotowski in 1985. Grotowski designated Richards his 'essential collaborator' in the research known as Art as vehicle. Through a 13-year practical apprenticeship, Grotowski transmitted to Richards what he called the 'inner aspect' of his work. In 1996, Grotowski changed the name of his Workcenter in Pontedera to Workcenter of Jerzy Grotowski and Thomas Richards to emphasize the vital, active role Richards played in the research. Richards is currently the Workcenter's artistic director.

5 Mario Biagini became one of the central contributors of the Workcenter of Jerzy Grotowski shortly after its founding in 1986. In 2000, he became the associate director of the Workcenter of Jerzy Grotowski and Thomas Richards. Along with Richards, Biagini was named the legal heir of Grotowski's intellectual property. He is the director of the Workcenter's Open Program.

6 The name of the school itself, Społeczne Liceum Ogólnokształcące Autorska Szkoła Samorozwoju (ASSA), which contains the word 'self-development', is indicative of the terminology circulating in Wrocław in the second half of the twentieth century. The term 'authors' does not designate a school for authors; it is meant to indicate that the school has no directors or principals, but 'authors' instead—it is 'authored'. It seems that the school's 'authors' were not sufficiently sensitive to the intimate relationship between authorship and authority, at least on a theoretical or textual level which, of course, cannot be divorced from practice. ASSA, founded in 1990 by Daniel Manelski and Darek Łuczak, is a 'democratic' school governed by students.

Its stated objective is to create the conditions for a comprehensive and holistic development of the individual. The school's philosophy emphasizes the importance of a young person's 'right to self-realization'.

7   All English translations of quotes appearing in Polish or other languages are by the author unless otherwise specified.

8   In 2004, Grzegorz Ziółkowski succeeded Zbigniew Osiński as the programme director of the Grotowski Centre, a position he held until 2009.

Jerzy Grotowski's lifelong research, while taking various forms and undergoing multiple transformations, is unified by a single underlying propulsion—the work on the self with and through the other. The present study pulls together threads of various aspects of Grotowski's broadly construed notion of self-development from various phases of Grotowski's research in order to begin to approach the totality of his complex understanding of human relationality and the self-realization of the human being.

While coming into (one's own) being through the other is at the heart of the Grotowski work, its realization is intricate and multifaceted. In this volume, I engage in a critical analysis of key aspects of Grotowski's notions and praxes associated with the work on self, including: the (re)discovery of essence through the process of active remembering; the exploration of vigilance understood as enhanced states of awareness and an active wakefulness which lead to acts of witnessing and testification; the vertically structured work on the refinement of energies; and, finally, the numerous and complex lines of transmission conceived as a multidirectional process of relationality with the (imagined) ancestor to the broadly construed 'twin'. While the present work explores these elements individually in order to elicit a fuller description and an in-depth analysis of each, all of these aspects are in reality various elements of one multifaceted and complex phenomenon of the work on oneself, which constituted one of Grotowski's most essential preoccupations. Through a critical and theoretical engagement with the conceptual framework that grew directly out of his research, I demonstrate the ways in which Grotowski's praxis constitutes a concrete and deliberate blurring of the boundaries of the self and other.

I begin in Chapter 1 with the consideration of Grotowski's work with memory which in the context of his research is always body-memory. In Grotowski's work there are at least two different types of memory work that emerge in two distinct phases of his research. The first is the use of body-memory undertaken during the Theatre of Productions phase. Here, the work with body-memory is used as a tool in the process of self-penetration and opening undertaken by the actor, in which memory serves as an instrument in the rediscovery of the impulses and intentions of a past moment. This process of rediscovery is integral to the freeing of creativity and tapping into the obstructed internal resources of the actor.

Another use of memory work, which becomes articulated in the phase of Grotowski's research known as Art as vehicle, is that which facilitates the rediscovery of essence. Grotowski's practice of active remembering, discussed at length in Chapter 1, functions as a tool in the search for one's essence, understood by Grotowski as the most intimate, precultural aspect of the self—as that which precedes difference and is at once the most singular and universal aspect of being.

Integral to Grotowski's work on theatrical craft, as well as other more broadly conceived work on the self, are heightened states of awareness, attentiveness or vigilance. While vigilance is a fundamental state and practice throughout all phases of Grotowski's work, in Chapter 2 I focus on the examination of a series of paratheatrical events explicitly associated with vigilance, such as *Night Vigil* and *The Vigil*, both conceived and carried out by Jacek Zmysłowski. I attempt a reconstruction of these scantily documented series of events, based on sparse archival materials as well as the oral testimonies of the organizers and participants of *The Vigil*, set against the background of traditional Polish and Eastern European practices and rituals associated with vigilance and the vigil. Furthermore, I argue that these states of enhanced conscious awareness, or vigilance, facilitated acts of testification or witnessing both on the part of the actor as well as the spectator. I explore the ways in which the performative act constitutes evidence of heightened awareness and perception that takes place within the actor, and argue that it is this very act of testification by the performer that subsequently transforms the status of spectator into witness.

Next, I turn to the description and analysis of the final stage of Grotowski's work known as Art as vehicle in order to consider Grotowski's conceptualization and praxis related to a vertically structured work on the self. In this last phase of research, Grotowski and his collaborators developed extremely precise performance structures deeply tied to what Grotowski considered archaic vertical structures, traces of which he found in various ancient traditions. These structures or performance opuses, as they were called, serve as precise tools in the refinement of one's energies. While Grotowski saw analogous tools in various traditional sources, for his own research he chose to work with Haitian songs and ritual movements, such as the *yanvalou*, as well as textual material from the Christian Gnostic tradition, such as the Gospel of Thomas and 'The Hymn of the Pearl', a poem from the Gnostic Acts of Thomas. In Chapter 3 I examine the deployment of these source texts along with ritual, song and movement in relation to Grotowski's notion of verticality. I extend this discussion to encompass Grotowski's conceptualization of human relationality, particularly vis-à-vis the image of twinship, which recurs both in the Gnostic literature selected by Grotowski and subsequently appears in performance work structured around texts such as *The Twin: Action in Creation*.

My discussion and analysis of Grotowski's view of human relationality extends to Chapter 4, in which I delineate the complexity and multidirectionality of transmission by examining Grotowski's real and imagined relationship with Haiti. It is in this chapter that I examine yet another strand of Grotowski's broadly construed understanding of ancestral relations and multiple lineages by considering his relationship with the Haitian Vodou priest Amon Frémon as well as Grotowski's work with the 'performative artefacts' of the Afro-Haitian line, which constitute the embodied practices associated with Vodou.

Methodology

My exposure to Grotowski has been long and gradual. However, it was not until embarking upon this project in the early months of 2009 that he constituted for me a scholarly object of study. For me Grotowski has always been a point of reference, someone I measured myself up to and against, an interlocutor as well as an imagined relative, someone who came before.

My long-term exposure to and relationship with Grotowski and his work holds both benefits and dangers. And while I vehemently oppose a stance that would assert that Polishness gives one a privileged understanding of Grotowski or his work, and find objectionable what seems to be a common practice of plotting oneself on the relative scale of closeness to the 'Master'—an act usually conducted to exclude others—I am not unaware of ways in which my status as a relative 'insider' positions me in relation to the object of this analysis. Here, I have in mind both the trust and openness with which I have been entrusted by Grotowski actors and collaborators. The knowledge of the man and his work has been conveyed to me not only through formal interviews, but often through long conversations, sometimes unsolicited, about individual experiences with

Grotowski. The relative accessibility to materials, public and private archives, and source languages has been extremely helpful in my research.

At this time there exists a large number of Polish-language articles and essays authored by Grotowski that have yet to be translated into English. In the context of this study, I have used existing English translations of Grotowski's work and my own translations of texts that have not yet been published in English. In translation I have tried to stay as close to the wording and syntax used by Grotowski as possible. As a result the English is at times a bit awkward. However, I have resisted a more elegant translation since this would require additional interpretation on my part and likely distort Grotowski's intended meaning. That is not to say that all translation is not always already an interpretation. However, my intention here is to provide as literal a rendering as possible. This approach reflects Grotowski's own preference for a more literal translation at the expense of more polished and at times even 'proper' usage of the target language.

While a genealogy of certain key terms deployed by Grotowski, such as essence, transmission, witnessing, verticality and so forth, is very important and warrants a project in its own right, it is not the focus of my current investigation. Grotowski read widely and was undoubtedly familiar with the ways in which these terms circulate in contemporary scholarship. However, his own understanding of terms was highly personal and grew directly out of his practical work. While I am careful to avoid providing simplified definitions of his key terms, it is my hope that the descriptive and analytical labour of this study begins to draft Grotowski's conceptualization of his working terminology.

For this project I have had access to the Grotowski Institute archive, selected materials from the Workcenter of Jerzy Grotowski and Thomas Richards, as well as the private photo collection of Grotowski actor and photographer Andrzej Paluchiewicz. In addition to conducting archival research, I have interviewed Laboratory Theatre actors, leaders, and participants of paratheatrical events as well as other Grotowski collaborators.

However, as a large anthropological literature on the subject attests, 'insider' status brings with it various challenges. For me, the relative proximity I had to Grotowski's Laboratory Theatre and its actors in my childhood as well as my subsequent exposure to his work through the Grotowski Centre during my formative years have deeply influenced my own development. This gradual and long-term acculturation to Grotowski and his work makes it at times difficult to distinguish between what I internalized of Grotowski at a young age and the impact of other influences. This early assimilation of Grotowski's work undoubtedly contributed to the fact that when rereading various Grotowski texts for the purposes of this writing, I found deep resonances between the tenets put forth and my own perception of reality even, or perhaps especially, when the assertions are not particularly popular within certain trends of contemporary US scholarship. While my perspective is that of a relative insider, this does not imply that distance and a critical stance cannot and does not exist.

My methodology, however, has been to approach this project in waves or layers. The first layer of research has been to enter into the consideration of various key themes in Grotowski's work, such as body-memory, vigilance and witnessing, vertical structures of development and transmission, in an attempt to understand by approaching, as closely as possible, Grotowski's own understanding and praxis of these themes. While informed by literature in the field of memory studies, as well as various theories of witnessing and transmission, I have been very attentive not to enter the project through the imposition of external theoretical frameworks onto Grotowski's work. First and foremost, my task has been to move towards ascertaining a clear picture of Grotowski's own theoretical formulations and practical work with and around these themes. It is only after taking this crucial step in my research that I am able to take a step back and put Grotowski in conversation with other theories of memory, witnessing and transmission and consider the implications that his practical research may have on these fields. This approach, however, is also reflective of Grotowski's own methodology encapsulated by his oft-cited dictum: 'Doubt before and after, but not during.'

While there is no dearth of written material on Grotowski, most of the literature either addresses one of the many phases of his work or moves horizontally through a description of these phases. The present study departs from such an approach by structuring its content thematically—or vertically—rather than chronologically.

The historical and political contexts within which Grotowski's work developed had an undeniable importance in shaping his research.[1] Grotowski's political astuteness becomes discernable in such tactical moves as having the Laboratory Theatre actors join the Communist Party, reasoning that the communist government could easily disband a theatre ensemble, but who would dare dissolve a communist cell? The inextricability of Grotowski's artistic practice and the sociopolitical context from which it emerged is made further evident in Grotowski's strategic evasion of state censorship—which concentrated mainly on literary texts—by placing an emphasis on the physical aspects of his work as well as the extended rehearsal periods. Grotowski's expert political strategies ensured the long-term viability of the Laboratory Theatre within the context of communist Poland.

While a comprehensive analysis of the reciprocal relationship between the artistic practice and the sociopolitical reality within which it emerged is beyond the scope of the present study, I would like to briefly unearth some of the political strands of Grotowski's own life and career as a counterpoint to the popularized misconception of Grotowski's work and theatre as apolitical.

Jerzy Marian Grotowski, the son of Emilia Grotowska née Kozłowska (1897–1978) and Marian Grotowski (1898–1968), was born in Rzeszów in southeastern Poland on 11 August 1933. His mother was a schoolteacher and his father a forest ranger and a painter later in life. In 1939, when the Germans invaded Poland, Grotowski, along with his mother and older brother Kazimierz (b. 1930), moved to the small village of Nienadówka, 12 miles north of Rzeszów. There his mother raised the two boys on a meagre teacher's salary while their father served as an officer in the Polish army, and later in the Polish army in exile in England. Marian Grotowski, who harboured strong anti-Soviet sentiments, never returned to Poland after the war but immigrated to Paraguay instead.

Grotowski's political activity began soon after the Second World War when, in 1946, the 12-year-old formed an underground, one-person anti-communist organization. While little is known about Grotowski's adolescent political imagination which prompted this contestatory gesture, several family sources reveal that the young boy commissioned a stamp with his last name and insignia, indicating the insurgent nature of this underground rebel entity. The old artisan who received this consignment informed on the boy and the young Grotowski was picked up and interrogated by the Polish secret police. Although the officer conducting the interrogation—having accurately assessed the low risk of threat that this 12-year-old held in relation to the communist state—told him to 'go home to his mother,' this startling encounter with the authorities shook up the young boy (Kazimierz Grotowski 2001: 17–18).

The thread of Grotowski's political activities re-emerges much later—albeit in a drastically altered form—around the time of his entrance examinations to the theatre academy. After the war, the Grotowskis moved back to Rzeszów and subsequently to Kraków, where Jerzy completed his high school education and, in September 1951, took the entrance examinations to the Theatre School. The examination committee granted Grotowski the following evaluation: physical appearance, C; diction, F; voice, B; expressiveness, C (Osiński 1986: 14). What saved him was the committee's consent to allow Grotowski to take the written exam, for which he received an A. Grotowski's political acumen is arguably already evidenced by his choice of essay topics. Out of three possible themes, Grotowski chose to respond to the exam inquiry that read: 'How can theatre contribute to the development of socialism in Poland?' (Osiński 1986: 14).

Beyond the strategic choice of essay topics to which the apposite response undoubtedly constituted the decisive factor that determined his admission to the theatre school, Grotowski was also member of the Union of Polish Youth (Związek Młodzieży Polskiej, ZMP), a communist organization. While membership of ZMP in itself was not necessarily indicative of one's political persuasion (membership was obligatory for all those who wished to attend the university or partake in other social privileges), all historical and archival sources reveal and substantiate that Grotowski was a true ideologue and sincere supporter of the Polish communist state. Already during the time of his studies at the State Theatre School in Kraków (Państwowa Wyższa Szkoła Teatralna, PWST), Grotowski published articles in the local press advocating for the socialist cause and promoting a nuanced understanding of social realism in art and theatre. In his first article published in January 1955, entitled 'The Little Red Balloon', Grotowski called on the authorities and people of good will to organize a space in Kraków that would emulate the legendary 'Little Green Balloon'—formerly a cabaret and place of meeting for literati, poets and artists. The change of balloon colour—to red—in the young reformer's vision is not insignificant. Grotowski, with his 'co-dreamers', imagined this space as a site for a great new centre for creative fermentation. He petitioned for this vision during the thirteenth session of the Cultural Council and insisted that the new Club of Young Creators formed by the ZMP be transformed into the 'Little Red

Balloon' aimed at a 'true attack against the remainder of the encrusted bourgeois atmosphere of our artistic community' (Grotowski 1955a: 2).

In his publications of this time, Grotowski accused the theatre community of cynicism, lack of courage and programmatic vision. He advocated socialist humanism, which he deemed as truly revolutionary, along with a vision of sociorealism which allows for artistic diversity. In an attempt to shed light on the potential variety of artistic trends within social realism, he cited examples from the Soviet theatre, arguing that the richness of sociorealistic art practice gives space to and is determined precisely by individual conceptualizations of theatre (Grotowski 1955b).

In June 1955, Grotowski graduated from the theatre academy and received a scholarship to study directing at the State Institute of Theatre Arts (Российский университет театрального искусства, ГИТИС or GITIS) in Moscow. Between 23 August 1955 and 15 June 1956, he studied there under the supervision of Yuri Zavadsky, who had in turn worked with Evgeni Vakhtangov. Even before his departure for the Soviet Union, Grotowski was known as 'a fanatic disciple of Stanislavsky' (Osiński 1986: 17). And while his intention was to study Konstantin Stanislavsky at the source, Grotowski gained more than he had expected when, during his Moscow studies, he discovered the work of Vsevolod Meyerhold (Osiński 1986: 18).

Zavadsky, the artistic director of the Theatre of Mossovet in Moscow, staged many patriotic Soviet plays and was well endorsed by the Soviet administration, as evidenced by the numerous decorations he received, including the state Stalin's Prize, Lenin's Prize and, on multiple occasions, the Order of Lenin. There is anecdotal evidence suggesting that Grotowski gleaned many political insights and stratagems from Zavadsky, who told his favourite student—before the latter's return to Poland—that he regretted being co-opted by the Soviet state and that the price he had to pay for his privileged existence was 'not worth it'.

After his studies in Moscow, Grotowski embarked upon a two-month trip to Central Asia. Upon returning to Kraków, in the fall of 1956, Grotowski's political engagement and activity grew to an unprecedented degree. He fantasized about a career as a politician, and was not far from achieving this desire until a traumatic event shifted the course of his life. Grotowski was quickly becoming an influential voice as one of the chief delegates of the radical faction of activists called the Revolutionary Youth Association (Rewolucyjny Związek

FIGURE 4: Wrocław, members of the Laboratory Theatre participate in a 1 May parade (1971/72). Photograph by Andrzej Paluchiewicz.

Młodzieży, RZM). As a 'combative revolutionary', Grotowski passionately proclaimed slogans calling for a democratization of public life and triumph over Stalinism at congresses and symposia. He advanced quickly up the union hierarchy and soon became Secretary of the Provisional Central Committee of the newly formed Association of Socialist Youth (Związek Młodzieży Socjalistycznej, ZMS).

Integral to Grotowski's early political activity was his participation in public polemics, which often appeared in the press. For instance, in response to an article by Paweł Dubiel asserting that ZMS is in grave danger from Grotowski's most radical line of thinking, which threatens the ideological and political unity of the People's Republic, Grotowski writes:

> Due to the affection that one might harbour toward Paweł Dubiel [. . .] I hurry to complete the list of my offences against the youth movement and the Polish People's Republic:
>
> 1. Under the rubric of intergenerational struggle, I castrate old men.
> 2. I gnaw on telegraph poles in order to introduce anarchy.
> 3. Every week, I build another tier onto the Palace of Culture.
> 4. At night when I step out for my evening walk, I greet fellow comrades with the words 'Good Day', in order to wreak ideological havoc.
> 5. I buy milk from housewives in order to lower the standard of living (1957: 5).

Beyond suggesting a boldness indicative of a sense of security within the sociopolitical schema, Grotowski's sarcastic remarks reveal a sense of humour not only in relation to himself but also—to a certain degree—to the social system within which he was operating.

However, his swift ascent up the party ladder was disrupted when, in the winter of 1957, Grotowski participated in a demonstration against the provocative liquidation of *Po Prostu*, a Polish weekly published by students and young intelligentsia engaged in a reform movement emblematic of the changes surrounding the 'Polish October', which signalled a change of the central authorities, liberalization of the system and release of political prisoners and clergy. During the demonstration Grotowski was bludgeoned with a club by the Motorized Reserves of the Citizen's Militia (Zmotoryzowane Odwody Milicji

FIGURE 5: Ludwik Flaszen. Photograph by Andrzej Paluchiewicz.

Obywatelskiej, ZOMO), a paramilitary police formation. The ZOMO used billy clubs to beat Grotowski—who had been suffering from chronic kidney disease—on his lower back. This brutal attack prompted utter disillusionment and extinguished Grotowski's idealistic visions of reform and therewith any hope for a political career. Grotowski re-immersed himself in the world of theatre and made his directorial debut in the spring of 1957 with Eugene Ionesco's *The Chairs*.

In an ironic and serendipitous play of chance Ludwik Flaszen makes the following pronouncement on Grotowski's theatre debut in his review of *The Chairs*: 'Kraków has not seen such a flop in quite a while, likely not since the time of the first sociorealist blotches' (1957). Flaszen, of course, is the theatre critic who two years later will invite Grotowski to direct the Theatre of Thirteen Rows in Opole and serve as the literary director of the provincial theatre, a function that he would continue to uphold in the Laboratory Theatre in Wrocław. Flaszen's role as the theatre's internal critic and Grotowski's personal devil's advocate is prefigured and can be clearly discerned in his critical stance towards the political status quo which he articulated in his book *Głowa i mur* (Head and Wall, 1958), a work which was banned by official state censorship of the People's Republic of Poland.

The creative and practical collaboration of these two men—Grotowski and Flaszen—informed by the confluence of the respective expertise that each brought from his engagement in political activity at opposing sides of the spectrum (Grotowski attempted to reform the system from within, Flaszen from the outside) made for a quarter century of very potent creative experimentation which often eluded state censorship and found ways to thrive in the exiguous economy of communist Poland. However, even with the collaborative resourcefulness of these two men, the Theatre of Thirteen Rows did not evade the continuous scrutiny of the state and frequent attacks from detractors. In July of 1963, Tadeusz Galiński, the minister of culture at the time, attacked the theatre in his quest to root out 'foreign' ideological influences in Polish cultural life. As a direct consequence of this attack, the Regional Party Headquarters (Komitet Wojewódzki, KW) cut the theatre's budget in half for the following year, which in effect meant that the Laboratory Theatre would no longer be able to exist in Opole. Grotowski fought back by setting in motion all of the theatre's allies. Newspaper articles appeared that attempted to intervene in the theatre's impending closure. A special commission on theatre was convened by the Ministry of Art and Culture to evaluate the activity of the Theatre of Thirteen Rows. But even the committee's positive resolution and recommendation for additional funding proved ineffectual. Grotowski's consequent decision to found a Basic Party Organization (Podstawowa Organizacja Partyjna, POP), the smallest unit of the Communist Party, was a desperate attempt to save the theatre. The reasoning of this move was absolutely on the mark—Grotowski rightly assessed the impossibility of the dissolution of a communist cell. However, despite popular legend and oft-cited anecdote, it is more likely that what actually saved the theatre was the move from Opole to Wrocław. The partnership forged between the monthly journal *Odra* and the president of the city of Wrocław provided the financial raft that allowed for the theatre to transfer its base to the larger university town and keep the operation afloat amid the country's political turmoil for the next 20 years.

The ways in which Grotowski and Flaszen 'worked the system' in order to keep the Laboratory Theatre, with its 10 to 19 (depending on the season) full-time creative staff rehearsing sometimes for a year at a time without any public performances, is testimony to a deep understanding of the sociopolitical realities in which they functioned. The work of fleshing out the various tactics and strategies deployed by the two men is yet to be undertaken, and will require a major archival research project with a team of researchers. Many sources point to the fact that Grotowski himself ordered the internal theatre archive to be destroyed. Much of the remains of the Laboratory Theatre archive are, in fact, not explicitly political in nature. A project attempting to reconstruct and analyse the political dimensions of the theatre's operation will necessitate both oral testimony and research in several official archives, including the Institute of National Remembrance (Instytut Pamięci Narodowej, IPN). The latter task presents pragmatic difficulties due not only to a lack of proper indexing but also, and more importantly, because of the controversial nature of the archive and its prosecutory powers.

In 'The Little Red Balloon', Grotowski argues against a simplistic and declarative political stance within theatre and artistic practice, which for him often implies turning art into a political treatise, placard or agitprop, and replaces 'harnessing one's own heart, a whole arsenal of artistic resources: the simplest, clearest means and made believable through the truth of human experience' (Grotowski 1955a: 2). Grotowski's performances from the Theatre of Productions phase, while—with some notable exceptions—not overtly political, were saturated with themes pertaining to the individual's struggle within society. The performances, and indeed the entire operation of the Laboratory Theatre, were deeply entrenched in the political economy of post–Second World War communist Poland. In light of Grotowski's youthful political ambitions and the traumatic events that led to their harsh suppression, one could see his choice of theatre as a life path as a tactical shift, an adjustment to the sociopolitical realities with which he was confronted.

Following the brutal attack by ZOMO, the site of Grotowski's political activity shifted and underwent a radical transformation. It was from this point onward that the primary terrain of struggle was transposed to a broadly conceptualized work on the self, which—within the theatrical context—implied the practical work of the actor. Years later, Grotowski would formulate the undercurrent of the political within his aesthetic practice and its ramifications thus:

You can always find allies, and you always find enemies to combat. You are faced with an extremely rigid social system. You must make your own way. You must find your own freedom within yourself. You must find your allies. [. . .]

Here is my attitude: I don't work in order to lay out some treatise, but rather to extend that island of freedom that I carry. My job is not to make political declarations but to make holes in the wall; things that have been forbidden to me must be permitted after me; doors which have been locked must be opened; I must solve the problem of liberty and tyranny in practical ways—that means that my activity must leave behind traces, examples of liberty. It's not the same as leaving complaints about the subject of freedom, such as 'Freedom is good. We must fight for freedom.' (And it's often the others who must do the fighting, etc.) [. . .] All that deserves to be chucked away with the garbage. You must actually get things done, and never give up but always press on, one step at a time. This is the problem of social activity through culture (Grotowski 1987a: 30–1).

The work on oneself understood thus, as an ethical and political praxis, permeates Grotowski's lifelong research, even while—for the reasons outlined above—it does not claim any overt political stakes. It is to the overview of the fundamental premises of this praxis associated with the work on oneself that I now turn. Because there exists a rather large literature on Grotowski to which the English reader can refer,[2] in the following pages I will limit myself to a brief overview of the various phases of his research integral to the understanding of the analyses contained in this volume.

An early pioneer in the field of environmental theatre, Grotowski's contributions to contemporary performance include a reconceptualization of the physical basis of the actor's art with an emphasis on the performer's obligation to daily training, as well as the exploration and refinement of a performance technique rooted in the principles of Stanislavsky's 'method of physical actions'. Early on, Grotowski articulated a need for a type of performance laboratory modelled after the Bohr Institute (of nuclear physics)—a forum for the investigation of the principles governing artistic creativity that would demystify the creative process. Grotowski's formulation of investigations into the actor's craft—while by no means scientific—were governed by certain 'objective laws'.

FIGURE 6: Jerzy Grotowski. Photograph by Andrzej Paluchiewicz.

The term 'objective' in Grotowski's terminology denoted observable facts with certain precise and determinable effects on the participant's state of energy.

Grotowski's work can be roughly divided into four phases: (1) Theatre of Productions (1957–69); (2) Paratheatre (1969–78) and Theatre of Sources (1976–82); (3) Objective Drama (1983–86); and (4) Art as vehicle (1986 to Grotowski's death in 1999). There are at least two threads that run through all stages of Grotowski's work. The first is a focus on the self-development of the individual—both as artist and human being. The second is an exploration of the potentialities of 'a meeting' between two or more people.

During the Theatre of Productions phase, Grotowski, in the role of theatre director, led his actors towards the accomplishment of the 'total act', an absolute disarmament by means of which the actor 'reveals [. . .] and sacrifices the innermost part of himself' (Grotowski 1969: 35). The actors of the Laboratory Theatre were not concerned with questions of character or with placing themselves in the given circumstances of a fictional role. Rather, their task was to construct a form of testimony drawing on deeply meaningful and intimate experiences from their own lives, articulated in such a way that this revelation could serve as a provocation for the spectator. For Grotowski, the core element of theatrical exchange was the 'perceptual, direct, "live" communion' between the actor and spectator (ibid.: 19). In *Towards a Poor Theatre* (published originally in English in 1968), Grotowski describes the *via negativa*, a process of elimination by which the theatre is stripped of its extraneous elements (costumes, make-up, scenery, music, lighting and so forth) so that theatre is defined at its core as that which takes place between the actor and the spectator. The method of *via negativa* was also envisioned to have a corresponding internal dimension, in which the process of stripping off and discarding the social masks amassed through acculturation would expose the core and essence of one's innermost being. Underlying this early work is the conviction that performance has the capacity to catalyse inner transformations. The process of self-development undertaken by the actor in the course of rehearsals and revealed in performance was intended to incite an analogous experience for the spectator.

While Grotowski's work drew on many theatrical and nontheatrical sources and traditions both within and outside Poland,[3] the lineage that Grotowski himself delineated and accentuated time and again is what he saw as a continuation of a direct line of the work of Stanislavsky, and particularly the last phase of the Russian director's research on physical actions.[4] Stanislavsky used the term 'physical actions' to draw attention to a new direction in his work, which began after he realized that emotions and emotional memory are not governed by the will.[5] Instead of his well-established line of questioning of what the actor *felt* in a given moment, which incidentally is the mode that made the biggest imprint on Stanislavsky-inspired acting methods in the United States,[6] Stanislavsky began to ask what the actor *did* in a given situation. The discovery of the involuntary nature of memory led Stanislavsky to explore the embodied dimension of memory including motor memories and the memory of the body. The method of physical actions that Stanislavsky began to develop at this stage of his research examines patterns of human behaviour at the level of 'micro actions', the morphemes of human behaviour (Fumaroli 2009: 206). It is precisely this point of research that Grotowski saw himself as carrying forward. Grotowski characterized Stanislavsky's understanding of physical actions in the following manner:

> In order to free the actor from the enforced search for emotions, which he [Stanislavsky] recognized to be inefficient, he used the term *physical actions*, even if for him these actions in reality included the *interior*

monologue (i.e. what we think), points of contact with others, reactions to others, and the associations between what we do and what we remember, consciously or unconsciously. But now he conjoined all this whole, living ensemble into the expression *physical actions*. He was convinced, and I share his conviction, that if—in the process of play—we discover what we did in life or what we might do in precise circumstances, the emotional life will follow all by itself, precisely because we are not trying to manipulate it (In Fumaroli 2009: 206; emphasis in original).

Grotowski stressed that while marking a new centre of gravity, the work on physical actions was by no means severed from earlier phases of Stanislavsky's research, which were deeply engaged with personal associations, memories and emotive reactions. However, in this latter stage of Stanislavsky's work the rediscovery of the inner life of the actor was approached through the body, which—by recreating what one did in a particular moment in the past—was thought to create the conditions for the reappearance of the emotional life of that moment.

Grotowski was clear that while he saw himself as continuing the final phase of Stanislavsky's work, his own work on physical actions was not Stanislavsky's 'method of physical actions'. It was a continuation of the work marked by important differences. Among them are the different understandings of notions such as organicity and impulse and the context in which physical actions are explored. While Stanislavsky examined physical actions in the context of the quotidian social life of the actor, Grotowski's interest was in physical actions and impulses situated—to borrow Eugenio Barba's term—in extradaily circumstances, or in what Richards calls 'a basic stream of life' (Richards 1995: 99). Grotowski also distinguished his understanding of impulses from that of Stanislavsky. Grotowski interprets Stanislavsky's notion of impulses interior to an action as being expressed by the eyes and face—the periphery of the body (ibid.: 94). Grotowski himself, however, sees the impulses themselves as morphemes of acting. Impulse, according to Grotowski, is something very subtle and rooted deeply in the body. And while the impulse does extend itself to the periphery of the body, it is conceived as something not entirely of the corporeal domain (ibid.: 95). Grotowski describes the relationship between impulse and a physical action in the following manner:

Before a small physical action there is an impulse. Therein lies the secret of something very difficult to grasp, because the impulse is a reaction that begins inside the body and which is visible only when it has already become a small action. The impulse is so complex that one cannot say that it is only of the corporeal domain (1997: 88).

What Grotowski understood as 'organicity' is also a point of departure from Stanislavsky's definition, which implied the natural laws of daily social life and their expression on the stage. For Grotowski, organicity signifies *a current of impulses* of a quasibiological nature that comes from 'the "inside" and goes towards the accomplishment of a precise action' (Richards 1995: 93). Impulses always precede physical actions. Moreover, the relationship between impulse and intention is crucial. Impulses are inextricably linked to an intent which becomes manifest in an appropriate and necessary kind of tension: 'In/tension—intention. There is no intention if there is not a proper muscular mobilization. This is also part of the intention. The intention exists even at a muscular level in the body, and is linked to some objective outside you' (Grotowski in ibid.: 96).

The intimate connection between intent and impulse—the way in which intention lives in the body—is crucial to understanding what Grotowski meant by indicating that the impulse is not solely of the corporeal domain. Further, while the body assumes a central position in Grotowski's work with memory, which I will focus on in Chapter 1, it never represents a physicality severed from the totality of the human being. The impulse is neither a purely physical action nor only a disembodied thought. The two are indissoluble and the subtlety of this intermingling is at the heart of Grotowski's work on physical actions throughout all phases of research.

Notes

1 The most comprehensive historical English-language accounts of Grotowski's research are Zbigniew Osiński's *Grotowski and His Laboratory* (1986) and Jennifer Kumiega's *The Theatre of Grotowski* (1987). For a study that specifically addresses Grotowski's research in the political context of Polish communism see Seth Baumrin (2009).

2   The most comprehensive English-language resource encompassing all phases of Grotowski's work is *The Grotowski Sourcebook* edited by Richard Schechner and Lisa Wolford (2001[1997]). Osiński (1986) provides an overview of Grotowski's Theatre of Productions phase and extends to the early paratheatrical work. Kumiega (1987) along with Tadeusz Burzyński and Zbigniew Osiński (1979) trace Grotowski's paratheatrical research. Lisa Wolford (1996) provides the most detailed description of the Objective Drama programme conducted by Grotowski at University of California, Irvine. Thomas Richards (1995; 2008) provides the greatest insights into the last two phases of Grotowski's research.

3   Osiński (1998) discusses the varied sources of Grotowski's work at length. An important precedent for Grotowski's Laboratory Theatre is the Polish laboratory for theatrical craft and pedagogy, Reduta, founded in 1919 in Warsaw by the actor and director Julisz Osterwa and geologist Mieczysław Limanowski. For a short English-language history of Reduta and its influence on the Laboratory Theatre see Osiński (2008).

4   Grotowski's own understanding of his research as a direct continuation of the last phase of Stanislavsky's work is significant because it reveals a great deal about his own inclinations and self-evaluation. However, it should by no means be considered as exhaustive or remain unquestioned. Richard Schechner points to the discontinuities and dissimilarities between Stanislavsky and Grotowski (2009).

5   Stanislavsky's notion of affective memory (*affectivnaia pamiat*), sometimes also referred to in English as emotion memory, can be traced back to French experimental psychologist Théodule-Armand Ribot (1839–1916) from whom he borrowed the term (Benedetti 2004(1982): 46; Carnicke 2009: 154). Affective memory refers to a human being's ability to remember previously experienced emotional states by recalling the accompanying physical sensations.

6   In 1925 Polish-born film director and actor Richard Boleslavsky, who trained under Stanislavsky at the Moscow Art Theatre, founded the American Laboratory Theatre and was later joined by Russian actor Maria Ouspenskaya. Boleslavsky's teaching relied heavily on the notion of emotion memory and—under the influence of his student Lee Strasberg—it became the cornerstone of the Method (Benedetti 2004(1982): 99). For a discussion of the history of Stanislavsky's notion and technique of affective or emotion memory in the United States see Sharon Marie Carnicke (2009: 148–54).

FIGURE 7: Jerzy Grotowski.
Photograph by Andrzej
Paluchiewicz.

CHAPTER I

Embodied Memory

Grotowski's Work on Personal and Ancestral Memories

In his work with the Polish Laboratory Theatre (1957–69), Grotowski used the memory of the body as part of a process of self-penetration and opening undertaken by the actor. In his endeavour to probe deeply into the layers of the actor's being, Grotowski sought to access pivotal moments of the actor's past life through the careful reconstruction of the position and movement assumed by the actor's body as well as the rediscovery of the impulses animating a crucial moment in the past.

In his later research, starting in the 1980s and culminating in the Art as vehicle phase, Grotowski examined the role of the body in the transmission of transgenerational collective memory. Tracing a particular line of ancient African songs through its diasporic trajectory, Grotowski sought to reconstruct the vibratory qualities of these songs through his work on the body. In so doing he gained crucial insight and practical knowledge about how embodied practice serves as a repository and vehicle of collective memory.

Grotowski's work with the memory of the body began in the initial stages of this research. In the Theatre of Productions phase he began to use the body as a vehicle for the reconstruction of personal memories and associations that simultaneously worked to facilitate a penetration of deeper layers of the actor's being while, at the same time, constituting material for the performance montage. In a 1966 speech delivered at the Skara Drama School in Sweden, Grotowski spoke of his understanding of memory in relation to the body:

> I have spoken much about personal associations, but these associations are not thoughts. They cannot be calculated. Now I make a movement with my hand, then I look for associations. What associations? Perhaps the associations that I am touching someone, but this is merely a thought. What is an association in our profession? It is something that springs not only from the mind but also from the body. It is a return towards a precise memory. Do not analyse this intellectually. Memories are always physical reactions. It is our skin which has not forgotten,

our eyes which have not forgotten. What we have heard can still resound within us. It is to perform a concrete act, not a movement such as caressing in general but for example, stroking a cat. Not an abstract cat but a cat which I have seen, with which I have contact. A cat with a specific name—Napoleon, if you like. And it is this particular cat you now caress. These are associations (1969: 185–6).

In Grotowski's work terminology, the term 'association' very often stood in the place of 'memory'. The two terms were often used interchangeably. However, Grotowski would more often use the phrase 'What is your association here?' to inquire about the memory that was beginning to surface. Richards recalls:

When [. . .] Grotowski said to me, 'Thomas, what was your association in that moment?' he was referring to a kind of little pearl hidden inside the action I had just done, a kind of living nucleus related to a personal memory. So, in the work situation, the term 'association' appeared in direct relation with memories. Was I ever asked in work, 'What was your memory in this moment?' I don't think so. In fact, 'association' in our work terminology was used much more often than 'memory'. I cannot remember Grotowski asking me in the work: 'What was your memory?' (2009).

At times, it is this very line of questioning that prodded the actor—and later the doer[1]—to become aware of an unconscious memory.

It is not absolutely clear how Grotowski approached the selection of particular memories in working with the actor. His statement 'Now I make a movement with my hand, then I look for associations' from the 1966 Skara speech seems to indicate that physical movement preceded the memory or association that might later be selected for elaboration and development. However, Richards proposes that, in fact, Grotowski did not work according to 'a system', implying that Grotowski very well may have used numerous approaches depending on the capabilities of the individual actor as well as the specific circumstances of the work situation (ibid.: 1).

The greater reliance on the body rather than the mind as the primary site and receptacle of memory found its expression in an intensely body-centred methodology. A key aspect of Grotowski's practical work of this period involved the detailed reconstruction of the position and movement of the body associated with a personal memory of the actor. This process involved a rigorous examination of the embodied dimension of select memory traces, chosen from the actor's past specifically to facilitate the return to an internal state conducive to self-penetration. The actor would be asked to work with attentiveness and precision to rediscover the bodily aspects of a given associative memory from the past.

Yet the reconstruction of the external form of the body was premised on more than merely the notion that the bodily exterior informs the internal state of the person in question. Grotowski's interest and investigation—throughout his lifelong research—was intently focused *on the impulses that precede the movement of the body*. The work's objective, therefore, was not solely limited to the idea that the reconstruction of the bodily form associated with a past memory would infuse the actor with the internal emotional and psychic life of that occasion. Rather, the emphasis was placed on the *rediscovery* of the impulses and intentions that animated that moment. This methodology assumes that it is possible to access pivotal moments or states of being that occurred in the past. However, the reaccession takes place in the 'here and now' and is therefore a production with new meanings and implications.

Grotowski's insistence on precision in the process of rediscovering the bodily position and actions associated with pivotal memories from the actor's past helped create a concrete physical score which would subsequently be inserted in the overall performance montage. Not only did the score function as a component of the theatrical performance, it also provided a clear structure for the actor to utilize in the work on the self. This framework was used in a way analogous to the ritual and performative structures present in various traditions, intended to guide the practitioner on the path of self-development.

Once having accessed particular states of being, a precise structure that one could follow would facilitate a return to the desired state or process. It is the codified structures of these ritual practices that ensure their efficacy. Although examples of these practices in various cultures abound, Grotowski's common references in this regard were, among others, to Haitian practices of Vodou, the Islamic devotional practice of *dhikr*, the ritual practices and songs of the Bauls of Bengal, and the practices of Zen Buddhism.[2]

Grotowski was well versed in the performative and ritual practices of many cultures both through his readings and travels.[3] And while he undoubtedly borrowed—or stole, as he liked to say—from diverse performance traditions, he liked to trace the lineage of his work and associate it most intimately with that of Stanislavsky. What differentiated Grotowski's work of this period from ritual practices such as Haitian Vodou, for instance, was his interest in the exploration of the intrapersonal, rather than interpersonal, systems of associations.

Grotowski's term *ciało-pamięć* (body-memory) first appears in print in 1979 in a text entitled 'Ćwiczenia' (Exercises) in the leading Polish scholarly journal *Dialog* (1979b).[4] This text, like much of the published material authored by Grotowski, is a reworked version of a talk—in this case, one given in 1969 to an international group of workshop participants. In a short introduction to the piece, the text's editor Leszek Kolankiewicz explains that Grotowski considered this talk to be a summation of his work on exercises for actors.[5] While Grotowski thought of this phase of work as finished, he did not intend to imply that the exercises could or should not be developed by others.

In this talk—after discussing Stanislavsky's notion of an actor's point of tension and adding his own notion of the actor's point of relaxation—Grotowski spends a substantial amount of time speaking about the ways in which conventionally understood training compartmentalizes the actor and blocks all possibility of individual creative expression. What is more, Grotowski locates body-memory—and that which he sometimes calls *ciało-życie* (body-life)—as precisely the locus and source of creativity for the actor. Body-memory is intimately linked with a line of living impulses that are at the root of the actor's possibility for luminescence (ibid.: 131).

The notion of luminescence is linked to the act of liberating the body. This process can be achieved through the practical realization of authentic reactions[6] which are rooted within the body. Everything that is outside, that is, 'the gesture', is the visible end of this process (ibid.: 132). Grotowski, with his usual disclaimer that his words are not to be used as a recipe in acting, asserts that, relatively speaking, the whole area of the lower spine—the sacrum, the base of the stomach—is the source of living impulses. However, what is crucial behind the idea of the exercises is not to manipulate or fabricate such impulses but to unblock. For whatever is achieved in the exercises will be carried over during actions. It is in this context that the notion of body-memory first appears:

> Our entire body is memory and in our body-memory there are formed numerous points of departure. If during the creative process

we concentrate on the sacrum [*krzyż*], we will block the memory of the body, body-memory. And because our whole organic basis of physical reactions is in a sense objective, and if it [the sacrum] is blocked during exercises, then it will be in the same degree blocked during actions [*działania*].[7] This block will then encompass all other originating points of body-memory (ibid.: 133).

Grotowski goes on to discuss the importance of detail and precision in the work. He asserts that in daily life reactions are detailed and precise. The idea, both in art and life, is not to limit the quantity of detail, because every act performed completely is detailed and precise. The danger of not working on precise details, Grotowski warns—using one of his favourite and oft-recurring images—is to fall into plasma. Later in the text, Grotowski returns again to his notion of body-memory: [8]

Body-memory. It is supposed that memory is something independent of the rest. In reality, it is different, at least for actors. It is not that the body remembers. The body itself is memory. That which has to be done is the unblocking of body-memory. If one orders oneself 'now I must slow down the rhythm, change the order of the details . . .' and so forth, one is not liberating body-memory. Precisely because one is ordering oneself. What is at work, then, is the thought. But if—keeping the precision of the details—one allows the body to dictate various rhythms, all the time changing rhythms, changing the order, taking as if from the air another detail, then who is dictating? Not the thought. But not chance either. This is connected to life. It is not even known how, but it was the body-memory. Or body-life? Because it goes beyond memory. Body-life or body-memory dictated what was to be done in association with experiences or cycles of life experiences. Or potentialities . . . ?

This is a small step in the direction of embodying our life through impulses. At the simplest level, for instance, certain details of movement of the hands and fingers transform—keeping the precision of the details—in the return to the past, to the experience of touching someone—as in making love, for instance—to an important experience, that occurred or that *should* take place. This is how body-memory and life-body manifests itself. [. . .] The detail exists but it is surpassed, it enters the level of impulses, into body-life. [. . .] Rhythm, the change of rhythm, the order. Next: life-body 'swallows'—and this happens of its own accord—the details that still exist in their external precision, but now burst as if from 'within' through living impulse. And what was possible to gain in this manner? We have liberated the seed: between the banks of details now flows the 'river of our life'. *At once spontaneity and discipline.* In essence, this is decisive (ibid.: 133; emphasis in original).

Body-memory, along with the larger notion body-life, is at the very heart of the creative potentialities of the actor. It is the unblocking of the flow of body-memory within a precise structure that frees the creativity and inner resources of the actor. Letting this body-life flow coincides with the liberation of the internal impulses, the confrontation with which is the real practice of the actor, according to Grotowski.

Tracing the gradual process of the development of exercises for the actor, Grotowski arrives at what he calls an 'organic acrobacy [. . .] dictated by certain regions of body-memory through certain intuitions of the body-life' (ibid.: 136). Therefore, Grotowski asserts, he has abandoned many domains and areas of his previous training research for what is essential, and that is the work on body-memory and body-life.

In Krzysztof Domagalik's 1994 film *The Total Actor: Ryszard Cieślak in Memoriam*, Cieślak—citing Grotowski—again reiterates that it is not that the body remembers but that the *body itself is memory*. While this statement may appear to lend itself to metaphorical interpretations, Carla Pollastrelli[9] warns against the poetic reading of Grotowski's terminology and concepts (2009). Pollastrelli argues that Grotowski intended his terms to be understood absolutely literally (2009). Richards' interpretation of the term body-memory is also very concrete:

I understand it as something that is very practical and literal. The body *is* memory. This is a very practical indication for an actor, for a human being. Sometimes we can think of memory as something conceptual, a kind of ephemeral series of images that exists somewhere in our heads, when, in fact, all of our experiences have been lived by our body (2009: 3).

FIGURE 8: Ryszard Cieślak in *The Constant Prince*. Photograph by Krzysztof Bednarski.

In this instance, body-memory is connected to the totality of life experiences that are encoded in the body. While this type of body-memory may be associated with a conditioning that takes place in one's life through acculturation, it is important to note that Grotowski's work with memory is aimed at the rediscovery of essence, a territory that precedes conditioning, which I will discuss more fully later in this chapter. In fact, Grotowski's work throughout all of the

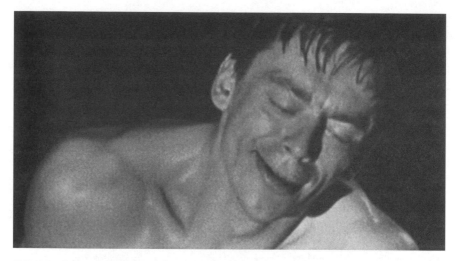

FIGURE 9: Ryszard Cieślak in *The Constant Prince*. Photograph by Andrzej Paluchiewicz.

phases of his research aimed to create the conditions in which a *de*conditioning would be possible.

In this view, the body contains both the memory of the conditioning as well as the state of being before this conditioning took place: certain moments in the past during which it was possible for the individual to drop all social masks and exist—if even momentarily—outside or beyond the conditioned self.[10] What is more, the body-memory functions as an indicator of the actor's current state. It is a concrete and observable dimension of the actor's being which can be used as an instrument in the process of deconditioning.

One prominent example that elucidates Grotowski's work with personal associations and body-memory is his collaboration with Cieślak on the title role of Calderón de la Barca's *The Constant Prince*. Calderón's play tells the story of Don Fernando, a Portuguese prince who—during the time of the Crusades—is compelled to give up the city of Ceuta to the Islamic Court of Morocco or remain a slave. The Constant Prince refuses to be ransomed and, reducing himself to abject poverty and servitude, abandons all those around him to die for a cause in which he alone believes.

While the narrative structure of Calderón's play is intelligible to members of the audience, the physical scores of the actors have little to do with the story unfolding on stage. During the performance, spectators watch as the Constant Prince undergoes imprisonment, interrogation, torture and flagellation. How-

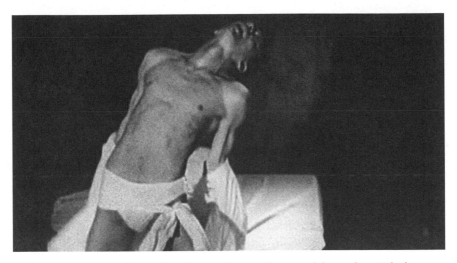

FIGURE 10: Ryszard Cieślak in *The Constant Prince*. Photograph by Andrzej Paluchiewicz.

ever, the actions that comprise this narrative sequence are based on Cieślak's personal association with a memory of a particularly joyous, ecstatic experience of his youth.[11] The words of the play uttered by Cieślak, framed by carefully constructed physical scores of other actors,[12] allow for a decoding of the logic of Calderón's play within the perception of the viewer. Although the content of Cieślak's personal association remains veiled from the spectators, the depth and authenticity of his experience is transparent.

In his essay 'From the Theatre Company to Art as Vehicle', Grotowski retrospectively analysed his work with Cieślak on memory. He stresses the nonarbitrary nature of the link between the actor's score and the memory fragment that is used in relation to it:

Yes, the cycle of the actor's personal associations can be one thing, and the line that appears in the perception of the spectator another thing. But between these two different things there must exist a genuine relation, a single deep root, even if it is well hidden. Otherwise everything becomes whatever, just casual. In the case of the work with Ryszard Cieślak on *The Constant Prince*, this root was linked to our reading— before we even started to work—of the *Spiritual Canticle* by John of the Cross (which rejoins the biblical tradition of the *Song of Songs*). In this hidden reference, the relation between the soul and the True—or, if you want, between Man and God—is the relationship of the Bride with her Beloved. It is this that led Cieślak toward his memory of an experience of love so unique that it became a carnal prayer (1995a: 123).

At this stage of his research, Grotowski was already attempting to couple personal associations with work on verticality, while simultaneously linking the work to a nonpersonal traditional source.

Grotowski revisits his work with Cieślak on *The Constant Prince* once more in an interview conducted by Marianne Ahrne in her 1993 film *Il Teatr Laboratorium di Jerzy Grotowski*:

> I worked for many months with Ryszard, alone, without any witnesses, even without his colleague actors, his partners in the play. For many months. And we referred to a memory in his life, a quite short memory of about forty minutes which was something extremely joyful. This memory was related to his teenage years when he had his first big love affair, that was—in the way that is almost possible only during your adolescence—something like . . . in between sensuality and prayer. At the same time, you can say that this happens in a 'no-man's-land', in this forbidden soil, this ground that doesn't belong to anybody, between prayer and sensuality. I would not say sexuality. Sensuality and prayer. We rediscovered, not as a reconstruction but as something alive, a way of taking flight. We looked for and rediscovered the smallest actions, the impulses of these re-membered moments. It was as if this teenager was re-membering, with his body, a liberation from the weight of the body, as if he was going to a land where there is no weight anymore, where there is no more suffering. But all this was made from impulses and actions, the smallest physical real actions of his memory, of a re-membered event that was rediscovered again—not reconstructed—for taking flight. Then, like a boat on a river, this thing was put onto Calderón/Słowacki's text (Ahrne 1993).[13]

In the interview, conducted in French, Grotowski uses the term *remémoriser*, which Mario Biagini, in his English translation of the transcript, has rendered as 're-membering'. The French *remémoriser* is as obscure as its closest literal English equivalent 'rememorize'. Grotowski, well known for his invention of a personal work terminology, often used words strategically to draw attention to something or to disrupt the automatic thinking and quotidian categorizations of the discursive mind. The term *remémoriser* signals an active remembering conducted by the body and distinguishes itself from a casual mental reminiscence. Richards describes his understanding of the term *remémoriser* in relation to his later work with Grotowski, which took place during the phase of Art as vehicle:

> *Remémoriser*. It's like to remind oneself again of something, in action. To remember. That's a word that one might even say to oneself within a performing situation. Often, while performing I say to myself, 'Thomas, remember, how was it? Like this? Like this . . .' In such a way, the accent is on the fact that when we approach a memory or an association underlying the acting score, we are remembering it. *Remémoriser* . . . Imagine. You go into the house of your childhood. It's here before you—you haven't been there for many years—and you walk through it again, and you rediscover 'ah, the table was . . . where was it? The table was here, yes.' This is to remémoriser. I am remembering how it was. I am calling it again to the present not only with my body, but with all of me. I am remembering, 'Ah, the table was here? Yes, the table was here. And the chairs, they were here. . . . No, the chairs were not here exactly, but here. And then I sit . . . and ah, yes, as I sit in my chair I remember a detail, the chair was low, so in fact my knees are bent in this way, they are a little higher than my hips.'
>
> What I did was to enter a process of questioning. I remember through action. It is an approach that can lead to an alive doing, because I am not trying to produce an effect, a result—I am also not trying to reproduce the effect of yesterday. One mistake of the bad actor—or an actor in trouble—is to try to reproduce the action of yesterday, or to produce once again what the director said was good, rather than entering again into the process of 'looking for'. This was an indication that Grotowski often said: 'You need to be *looking for*.' To keep looking for. Even when you are finding, keep looking for. So, when our acting or 'doing' is alive in one of our performing works, in fact, what we are doing is related to the term remémoriser (2009).

Richards' description of the process of active remembering serves as a concrete and precise illustration of what the practical engagement entailed in the work with memory initiated by Grotowski.

Afro-Haitian Vibratory Songs and Transgenerational Memory

Grotowski's later work, starting at least as early as the Theatre of Sources period, reveals a slight shift of emphasis in relation to memory, which begins to transcend the realm of the personal. Grotowski had already begun to investigate the transgenerational transmission of collective memory in the research conducted under the auspices of the Objective Drama programme at the University of California, Irvine. The conduit for this work became the songs rooted in the ancient traditions of various cultures.

Although one group in the programme, led by James Slowiak, concentrated exclusively on the vocal repertoire of the American Shaker tradition, the songs that Grotowski would continue to explore in subsequent phases of his work were rooted in the rituals of Afro-Haitian vibratory songs. His interest in the ritual tradition of Haiti had been long established. Before his exile from Poland after the imposition of martial law in 1981, Grotowski travelled to Haiti and worked with the rural arts community of Saint-Soleil led by Jean-Claude 'Tiga' Garoute and Maud Robart.

Grotowski's long collaboration with Saint-Soleil began with an invitation for them to take part in the Theatre of Sources in Poland.[14] The research attempted to reconstruct ancient vibratory songs connected to the Afro-Caribbean line of ritual practice back through its diasporic trajectory.[15] The intent was not only to preserve and repeat the melodic lines but also to recreate the vibratory qualities of these songs through physical work involving ritual movement. The work on ancient songs provided a physical and vocal structure along which more ephemeral work was constructed. It involved the refinement of energies from the lower, more carnal and vital, to the more subtle.[16] This more refined energy would then be reconnected to the dense and vital energy once again.

The construction of this structure—seeds of which can be seen in Theatre of Productions—has sometimes been referred to by Grotowski as the science of 'yantra' or 'organon'. In his 1987 article 'Tu es le fils de quelqu'un' (You Are Someone's Son), Grotowski describes yantra as an instrument possessing the precision of a surgeon's scalpel which, when applied, can connect one to the laws of the universe and nature:

> These are instruments which are the result of long studies. You not
> only need to know how to construct them, as with certain types of

dance and singing which have a certain objective effect on you, but you also need to know how to use them to avoid committing stupidities, and to reach a totality, a fullness (1987a: 37).

In the latter stages of his work, Grotowski used traditional songs as material for the distillation of yantra. He distinguished between what he called 'songs of quality' and the popular songs of a given culture. Songs of quality are those that are rooted in the ethnic or religious traditions of a culture and carry with them specific and complex patterns of vocal vibrations (Wolford 1996: 40). The Afro-Caribbean songs, with which Grotowski worked, constitute very sophisticated yantra and are capable of producing a profound inner effect on the participant (ibid.: 41). The vibrations of these songs can only be rediscovered and activated through the work with the body and its resonators.

Referencing Grotowski, Lisa Wolford Wylam[17] speaks of ritual songs as performative artifacts that allow the practitioner to embark upon a journey towards the beginning of a song, which allows the discovery of the 'first' singer within one's own body: 'Such a process of investigation is rooted in the premise that elements of knowledge are somatically encoded in the artifact itself and can be decoded by the attentive and receptive performer' (ibid.: 124). Although this type of journey necessarily precludes an experience that might be identical to that of an ancestor, Wolford Wylam notes that what can emerge is a dialogic relationship between the performer and the experience encoded in the artefact.

In his work, Grotowski would often suggest that a performer approach memory work through the encounter with source material of her own cultural and performative tradition. Sometimes he would suggest that the memory exercise be accessed through a precise detail, such as the memory of a photograph or the particular gait of one's ancestor. With this detail as a point of entry, the performer could begin to discover traces of 'somebody ancient' in her own body (ibid.: 51). Grotowski describes this palimpsest of embodied memory:

Who is the person singing the song? Is it you? But if it is a song of your grandmother's, is it still you? But if you, with your body's impulses, are exploring your grandmother, then it's neither you nor your grandmother who is singing: it's you that's singing as you explore your grandmother, that is to say, you are exploring your grandmother/ singer. Perhaps you go further back toward some time and place difficult to imagine, when someone sang this song for the first time . . . You have the song, you must ask yourself where it began (1987a: 38).

Grotowski's interest in 'sources' and 'beginnings' is already evident in the early stages of this work in Poland. Laboratory Theatre literary director Ludwik Flaszen is quoted as saying, 'We are not moderns, but traditionalists through and through [. . .]. It just so happens that the most startling things are those which have already been. [. . . We do not] want to discover something new but something forgotten' (in Osiński 1991: 112). Many years later Grotowski would mark the correlation between a discovery and memory:

Each time I discover something, I have the feeling it is what I recall. Discoveries are behind us and we must journey back to reach them. With the breakthrough—as in the return of an exile—can one touch something which is no longer linked to beginnings but—if I dare say— *to the beginning*? (2001a: 379; emphasis in original).

The notion of somatically encoded knowledge in which Grotowski's work is rooted, and which is operative in the above quote, relates further to certain strands of current scientific research.

It is difficult to assess the exact weight that Grotowski placed on scientific studies which might have had direct bearing on his practical research. On the one hand, the Laboratory Theatre itself was modelled on the scientific exemplar of the Bohr Institute. Moreover, Grotowski was very keen on discussing various scientific theories with his brother Kazimierz Grotowski, a professor of nuclear physics at the Jagiellonian University. On the other hand, it is clear that scientific research did not constitute an ultimate or uncontested authority for Grotowski. It is my contention that Grotowski negotiated between scientific and 'nonscientific' data.

While Grotowski did not use scientific terminology in framing his research, one can see how the recent findings emerging within the field of behaviour genetics could corroborate his explorations. Behaviour genetics involves the study of the ways in which genetic inheritance (genotype) and environmental experience jointly influence physical and behavioural development (phenotype).[18] What within this field is called the 'active gene-environment correlation',[19] and characterizes a scenario in which someone with a certain trait actively seeks support of this trait with others sharing it, could be seen as analogous to the conditions of work created by Grotowski for an individual performer in relation to the performative practice and a master teacher.

Richards, who began working with Grotowski in the Objective Drama programme in UC-Irvine, was initially assigned to the group led by Robart, which involved work on Haitian vibratory songs. Describing this experience in an interview conducted by Wolford Wylam, he recalls:

> When I heard the songs of Haiti, the traditional songs, it was like hearing the voice of my grandmother, whom I've never before heard sing. My grandmother's line on my father's side comes from the Caribbean; his parents come from Jamaica. During the two weeks when I heard these songs, it was like . . . touching in me something that had really never been touched up to that point. It's hard to explain, but even the melodies, this kind of sound and its vibration—which in that moment gave me the feeling I was hearing a tree sing—was shocking (Richards 2008: 2).

On the one hand, there is a clear link in Grotowski's work between the performer and the genetic line of his ethnic and cultural inheritance; Grotowski's frequent suggestion that a performer work with the source material of his own tradition seems to suggest this. Moreover, in the same interview Richards continues:

> My mother is white; my father is black. Half of my heritage comes from European culture, and half from African. Though my skin is a lighter color, in my physicality there is something of my father's line, the African line. I grew up in New York City, educated in a Western way, and something in me that I associated with this African line related to a special kind of fluidity and continuity of movement, the flow of vitality through the movement, which I would later discover to be a rich and creative channel for me. This had to a great extent been blocked, not yet discovered. Grotowski began to look to unblock this through practical work and also through conversations with me, in order that I might begin to accept in the working situation this resource in the body (ibid.: 4).

Nevertheless, the fact that before his death Grotowski officially declared Richards and Mario Biagini to be his 'universal heirs' implies that he did not understand transmission to be confined within clearly circumscribed and exclusive ethnic and cultural traditions. This notion of oral patrimony is not bound to a particular line of cultural inheritance. Similarly, in all phases of Grotowski's research, although working with material from one's tradition was suggested, performers also commonly worked with sources from outside their own culture.

Grotowski's lifelong work was deeply engaged in the potentialities of performance as a form of embodied transmission. In attempting to decode the performative artifacts of ancient ritual practice, Grotowski sought to penetrate the embodied knowledge of ancestral traditions connected with precise structures, or yantra, which facilitate a method of deep knowing. Grotowski sought to revalorize oral and embodied transmission. This emphasis is not only visible in the direction of his practical work but in the daily choices of transmitting his own knowledge, which included a preference of talks over publications, as well as an insistence that no participants use recording devices or even take notes at his lectures.

Grotowski explained the he discouraged note-taking because it prevents participants from being fully present and attentive to the moment. While taking notes one is preoccupied by the process of writing. Further, taking notes creates a false impression that it will be possible to access the knowledge being transmitted through the very archive being created. Grotowski often insisted that the film documentation of his work—and particularly that of the Art as vehicle phase—not be shown without the presence of either himself or Richards, because he believed that oral explanation and commentary were necessary to contextualize the work. Perhaps this restriction is linked to his conviction that, in performative as well as ritual forms, the imitation of that which is exterior leads solely to the construction of the representation of a form, and not to the penetration of its intent.

A Bridge Made of Memory:
Personal Memories in the Domain of Art as vehicle

In the *Heart of Practice: Within the Workcenter of Jerzy Grotowski and Thomas Richards*, Richards speaks at length about the ways in which memory and body-memory figured in his work with Grotowski. He describes a particular instance in which a past memory is recovered through Grotowski's recognition of organicity appearing in Richards' movements during the development of *Main Action*.[20]

Grotowski was watching a draft of *Main Action*, and I had a small fragment in which I was walking, carrying an object for another actor.
Grotowski stopped us. He said there was something in my work, in
what I had done. For me this was strange because I had just been
walking. He said, no, there was organicity, the seeds of organicity in
me in that moment. He asked what my association was, what I was
thinking as I walked, for whom I was walking. . . . As he questioned
me, a memory came to me about a time in my youth when I was carrying an object for my father in the hospital. I wrote down the memory
in my notebook (ibid.).

Here, Grotowski's recognition of the seeds of organicity and his consequent
inquiry led directly to the discovery of a memory associated with a particular
way of moving. The physical movement of the doer precedes the work with
personal memories or associations. It is the kernel of organicity that functioned
as a connective tissue that linked Richards' way of walking within the performative structure to a specific instance from his past.

What is crucial to recognize here is that it is the *intention* that informed
Richards' way of walking—while carrying an object for his father—that is integral to what Grotowski perceived as organicity. What is more, the memory that
was recovered and, subsequently, came to constitute an associative part of the
doer's physical score allowed him to reaccess this organicity and fluidity in
future repetitions of the score. It is possible to discern the double role of memory at play here. First, memory functions as a doorway into a moment in the
past that creates the possibility of infusing a present performative action with
an aliveness and organicity that informed the past. Second, the memory—when
attached to the physical score of the doer—assumes the role of a *reminder* and
provides a mode of re-entering the desired process of vitality, which in turn
facilitates a quality of presence and readiness that is indispensible to the work.

During the Art as vehicle phase of his research, Grotowski also approached
work with memory by selecting a particular memory from the doer's past and
developing an acting proposition around it. Richards, whose role by that time
had progressed to that of a work leader, describes how he assisted Biagini in
developing an acting structure involving a song Biagini had heard while living
on a farm as a child. In his conversation about the acting proposition with
Richards, Biagini remembered a specific time from his childhood, which he

began to investigate with his body and voice. Richards, who was acting as the outside eye, observes:

> I saw that when he remembered in action those moments from his youth, something really changed. His way of looking became more alive, with a specific way of questioning his mysterious object. He was really remembering that specific day on the farm. His body became like the body of a seven-year-old, with all its unique tempo-rhythms (ibid.: 81).

Here again, the memory provides an opening and a connection to an aliveness experienced in the past, which can be developed through investigative work conducted with the body and the voice around this particular memory fragment.

It is through this very work with Biagini that Richards began to gain practical insight into what Grotowski had perceived as alive in the work on physical actions—a quality that was used in contradistinction to the mechanical. The recognition of the 'alive element' that Grotowski had earlier attempted to transmit became more visible to Richards gradually as his practical sensitivity grew. Richards describes this recognition as the perception of something that has the quality of a substance, with a perceptible radiation emanating from it. It is this quality that he gradually began to recognize not only with his eyes but with his entire body, as if his skin was sensing and perceiving the quality of aliveness (ibid.: 80).

It is not only the faculty of recognition of aliveness that is closely tied to the body; it is also the embodied dimension of research that enables the doer to access a vitality which may have been experienced in the past and since forgotten. This way of looking—questioning with the body and the voice—is a way of active remembering and relearning that enables vitality to surface in the work. Richards continues to describe his work with Biagini:

> And sometimes he remembered a way of singing, how he had sung on the farm, into a shaft. It was as if he was asking with his voice what was at the end of the shaft. [. . .] It was an important moment in the work, because I started to see: yes, there is something alive; *that* is alive (ibid.: 81; emphasis in original).

This level of work—the rediscovery of vitality and organicity—is the primary labour undertaken by the doer and lays the groundwork for the inner aspect of the work on the transformation of energy, which I will address at length in Chapter 3. At the level of vitality, a precise memory has the potential of functioning as a way of accessing a reservoir or pool of energy that the doer once had access to but has become contracted as a result of life experiences. The work facilitates the rediscovery of forgotten human potentialities.

The physical and vocal structure, to which the personal memory fragments become linked, functions as a reminder that one can return to again and again, in order to refocus and reconnect to resources that might have become obstructed. When a doer encounters a discovery in the work, she must retrace her steps by analyzing the process that led her there and consequently create a structure that might allow her to return, develop and refine a discovery.

The analytical work involved in this process is characterized by Richards as follows:

> If I try to relive an experience that arose from an act, I immediately see that I cannot just relive it. I must analyze: what was I doing that brought me to touch that experience? What was I *really doing*? What was my specific line of actions? For example, yes, I sang that specific song with a precise flow of sonic resonance. But what were my intentions while doing? What was I thinking? Was the discovery related to a specific memory? How was my body in the act of doing? (ibid.: 74; emphasis in original).

Richards acknowledges that no experience can ever be repeated exactly; what is important here is not the exact replication but a return to a particular directionality in action, albeit within a specific and repeatable structure. It is within the process of a continuous and active searching and rediscovery that the potential lies for infusing the score with aliveness and organicity.

In the domain of Art as vehicle, work with memory is approached in different ways and has multiple applications. At times, work with memory functions as a mode of reconnecting to or rediscovering concrete moments from the past that are more closely aligned to the doer's potentialities. The doer's attempt to reconnect to those moments, and by extension to the potentialities that might have become obstructed in the course of one's life, instigate an active remembering which is inseparable from Grotowski's understanding of knowledge and the process of its discovery.

Grotowski defines 'Performer', in an essay originally written in 1990 bearing that title, as 'a man of knowledge' (2001a: 376). The Polish *człowiek poznania*, from which 'man of knowledge' is derived and which stands in parentheses in the English translation of the text, has a whole dimension of connotations that do not carry over into the English rendering. First, the Polish word *człowiek* is not gendered and is closer to its English equivalent 'human' or 'human being'.[21] More importantly perhaps, the Polish word *poznanie* is a noun formed from the verb *poznać*, which denotes not only study or the process of knowledge acquisition, but also a recognition or a coming to consciousness. Poznanie contains within it the verb *poznawać*, an imperfect form indicating an unfinished or continuous action. Therefore the noun *poznanie* carries strong connotations that point to the *process* of getting to know, of recognition and discovery, rather than knowledge as an object of acquisition.

Consequently, *człowiek poznania* is not, as the English rendering might suggest, one who is in possession of knowledge; rather, it is the person who is actively engaged in a continuous search for knowledge and discovery.[22] As Grotowski is quick to point out, *człowiek poznania* has at his disposal '*the doing* and not ideas or theories', and 'knowledge is a matter of doing' (ibid.). In this work, memory functions as a tool, a means or a vehicle for rediscovery. Richards uses other imagery in describing his work with memory: 'In this way I had a bridge, not a bridge towards a memory or a recollection, but a bridge made of memory' (2008: 104).

In the matters of doing—in Grotowski's own praxis—the active search for knowledge is closely linked to work with memory and the rediscovery of something lost or forgotten. At times memory figures in an interesting way as a longing, which indicates a lack within the doer. In this instance, memory functions as a reminder for the doer that there is something forgotten that needs to be found. Richards describes a continuity of the presence of what he calls one's 'core' as a point of departure towards the 'inner action', the core being 'a part that can feel a special longing, as if it remembers something that it lacks. It has a desire for plentitude' (ibid.: 64–5).

Here, as in other cases, forgetting is an integral part of active remembering, the other side of the coin necessary for the doer to realize that she needs to return to the process of active remembering. The experience of a lack and longing creates a stimulus within the doer to rediscover that which has been forgotten.

On Ancestral Memories in Art as vehicle

In addition to the process of excavation of moments experienced in the past undertaken by the doer, the domain of Art as vehicle contains another aspect of practice that involves memories of nonlived events. In the section of the essay 'Performer' entitled 'What I recall', Grotowski writes, 'One access to the creative way consists of discovering in yourself an ancient corporality to which you are bound by a strong ancestral relation' (2001a: 386). One point of entry to discovering this ancestral corporality is through the exploration and discovery of someone other, an ancestor of whom one still has a living memory. Richards gives a hypothetical example of how this exploration might look in practice:

> I sit down at this table and I lean forward but as I'm doing this there is an 'as if' involved. I'm doing this 'as if' it was my father in a specific instance that I'm remembering. Through action I am asking myself how his body tended towards the table as he picked up his pen to write that note to my mother that I saw him write (2009).

The deployment of the 'as if' in the process described by Richards allows the doer to explore the corporality of a *known* ancestor using specific memories.[23] This exploration might take a visual memory as its point of departure but will soon involve an embodied exploration of the exact positioning of the ancestor's body, the angle of the ancestor's spine, her age, the ancestor's relation and reaction to the other people in the memory. Alongside the active bodily search of the doer is a simultaneous letting go, a submission to the corporality of the remembered ancestor: 'I gently let the corporality of that person from my family come into me. [. . .] I let myself remember through doing the small actions of the person' (Richards 2008: 17).

Through the embodied exploration of somebody known, the doer may gradually extend the search for the corporality of someone unknown from the more distant past. This exploration does not lead to a literal remembering or embodiment of one's particular ancestor or an archetypal ancestor. It is, rather, an investigation conducted through an inquiry of 'how it might have been'. The Stanislavskian 'as if' is extended here to include an imagined line of ancestry reaching very far back. However, Grotowski asserts that through this mode of research one can 'arrive very far back, as if your memory awakes' (2001a: 379). The 'as if' in this contention implies that even though the memory may not be a literal one, *it is experienced by the doer as a memory*. Richards corroborates this idea through the testimony of his practical experience in the work: 'It's as if the soul meets something, something touches it, fills it. And strangely enough, it can be perceived as a sort of memory' (2008: 105).

In this aspect of the Art as vehicle work, memory functions as a tool in at least two ways. The work with the doer's personal memories serves to unearth deep potentialities and expand the receptivity of the doer through the remembrance of a time when one was closer to certain inner resources. The linking of these memory fragments to the doer's score is not arbitrary, but must contain a deep connection or resonance for the doer. The doer does not have to focus on the personal associations if the work is going well; however, memory-bridges are there—embedded in the score—and can be accessed as needed.

The memory-bridge of actual events remembered is coexistent with another level of memory work, which begins as the doer advances in the work. This more complex exploration involves the use of memory as a tool but in relation to nonlived events. As Richards stresses again and again, Grotowski had no 'system' and employed various strategies at this level of work, as he did in earlier phases of research.

There are at least two approaches that Grotowski used in accessing what he termed 'ancestral memories'. He proposed a series of embodied explorations that were structured along the same hypothetical line of inquiry as the work with personal memories. That is, he would ask the doer to imagine what the corporality of one's more distant ancestor might have been like. Again, this exploration was not solely mental but, rather, required research conducted with the body, the mind and the heart of the doer. The emphasis, as always, was on the body but with the implicit understanding that the body is not severed from other aspects of the doer's being. In short, this line of investigation is meant to be carried out with the totality of one's being.

In the exploration of ancestral memories, Grotowski proposed more than a single line of questioning that asked about the hypothetical being or corporality of the ancestor. In his work with Richards, he also suggested posing the question: What might I have been like, generations and generations ago? It is an exploration of oneself through the other and the other through oneself.

Another mode of approaching the ancestral corporality deployed by Grotowski was from the 'outside in'. That is, with certain collaborators he explored the effect that the external bodily form would have on the internal state of being. In the case of his individual work with Richards, the two explored ways of standing and the effect of certain stances on the doer by reconstructing the external bodily form from select photographs of African warriors:[24]

> You see in that film [*Downstairs Action*], in many moments of the singing process, I am standing in a specific way, with the knees bent and the spine very strongly arched. This way of standing, a precise way of standing—that was not pleasant, it was difficult—put a kind of, not stress but . . . accent in the spinal column, which created a kind of active tension in the body. This had an effect on me. We discovered that this way of standing somehow aided a vitality that was awakening in me through the songs, a living stream of impulses that could sustain and go with the process that the songs brought to life. We were trying this way of standing as an experiment. Together we looked at certain photographs of warriors in Africa, studied specific ways of standing, and then in work I tried to discover them in my body and flow of doing. In fact, it was not just one way of standing. We saw that for me these ways of standing interacted with the songs in a potent way. Of course, such an approach is personal. As we were singing, we saw how the songs and the ways of standing would impact me as an individual (Richards 2009).

What might be characterized as a more formal exploration of the ritual body and its objective effects on the doer, in this case Richards, introduces a different repertoire of bodily positions, stances and possible movements which have the potential of augmenting the hypothetical explorations conducted by the mind-body of the doer.

While work with ancestral memory was conducted at all phases of the work on Art as vehicle, there were particular moments when an emphasis was placed on this line of research. For instance, one period that involved intense research on ancestral memory was conducted through work on *Remembering Action*, which started in the winter of 1986 and 1987, shortly after members of the Workcenter moved from their temporary work space in Teatro Pontedera to Vallicelle, the space in which their work is carried out to this day. Work on *Remembering Action* lasted for roughly one year and began as an intense one-on-one process that Grotowski conducted with Richards; eventually two more doers were brought into the Action. Richards recalls:

It was called *Remembering Action* because of the approach that Grotowski was taking with me at that time. What I needed to do somehow was to remember—how to say—something buried deep inside me. I don't mean just psychologically, but almost encoded in me. The approach was that inside me, inside my being, my body, all of me, there was already a cycle of actions: the needed way of standing, the needed way of sitting, the needed ways of walking and contacting others, the simple performative elements that can go with the songs and help them lead towards a profound experience. We approached work as if these simple performative elements, that were very precise, already existed, inside. So, the elements of that Action appeared from a kind of going back towards something that was as if 'me' let's say generations and generations ago.

When we were working it was as if the active question was: How might Thomas have been in another circumstance, a long time ago? It was like to reach back asking body-being what it wanted to do, how it wanted to react, to sing/play, to sing/look for contact. So there was a kind of memory awakening, but it was not a memory from childhood, but rather related to my great-grandfather who I never met, let's say, or to my great-great-great-grandfather on the African side of my family. How might he have been doing? I mention this about great-grandfather as an example. We never really approached work through that specific association. It was rather through a kind of questioning: 'How might I have been doing in that other time, and how I might be doing, now?' It was like creating a bridge of precise actions, through which you're actively looking to go very far back, and also to create the present (Richards 2009).

What Richards is articulating is a spatially and temporally complex experience of self-discovery and realization. The experience is a rediscovery of that which is encoded in the totality of the human being. It is a rediscovery grounded firmly in the here and now and simultaneously deeply connected to that which came before; that which came before is encoded in the body of the doer, as if the body was a living artefact containing the imprint of all that preceded its being in the here and now.

However, this coding is not limited to the cultural conditioning of one life-time but extends back through one's imagined ancestral line all the way to the origin, the beginning. This is experienced as a deep connection that finds its expression in extremely precise performative actions. The realization of one's own potential takes place in the here and now and shapes the present moment but is concurrently experienced as a movement back in time to reconnect to one's roots. All of this is lived as a memory, as a rediscovery of something one has already known and experienced.

While the notion of an original or first beginning is implied, the beginning always also signifies the present moment, which must be experienced as a beginning constantly renewed. Being in the beginning is closely linked to the notion of aliveness. Organicity, aliveness, being in the moment and remembering are all inextricably interwoven. Richards discusses the ways in which the song functions as a means of remembering—as a link with the past, but also in its function as a mode of remembering to be in the now, in the beginning, which must be continually renewed. The latter function of the song is similar to that of a parameter, which indicates whether one is alive and present: '[T]he song is alive and you know and you see, and it's objective because people—who have the capacity, not everybody has this capacity of sensing the life—they can sense now it's alive, *now this person is in the beginning. He's living, he's remembering*' (ibid.; emphasis added).

The song's aliveness, which can be sensed by someone who has developed the faculty for this kind of perception, serves as an indicator that the doer is alive in the present moment. This being in the beginning—in the here and now—is also identified by Richards as a remembering, thereby linking it to another beginning in the past, and by extension to an archetypal beginning.

Essence and Being

In 'Performer', Grotowski points to the etymological relation between essence and being. He understands essence as that which precedes socialization and acculturation and believes that it is possible to discover and return to essence through performative work. This process can be seen as an inner *via negativa*, in which the doer discards internal masks until they reach a constituent substance of their being. It is a form of distillation which for Grotowski assumes an objective character; for the reality that underlies phenomena can be more clearly perceived as the body begins to move closer to essence.[25] In the context of the same essay, Grotowski discusses the passage from what he terms *body-and-essence* to *body of essence*. Body-and-essence is a transitional state in which a particular kind of organicity enters into an osmotic relationship with essence and the two become temporarily indissociable. Here, Grotowski gives the example of young warriors who lived in the villages of Kau in Sudan in the 1970s. After Zeami, he describes this state as a product of *the flower of youth*.[26] It is possible, asserts Grotowski, to transform this transitory state into a permanent one through a personal transmutation. This, he believes, is the challenge set before everyone, but how we answer this call is highly individualized. By linking one's individual process to essence, Grotowski argues, it is possible to 'catch his process. Adjusted to process, the body becomes non-resistant, nearly transparent. Everything is in lightness, in evidence. With *Performer*, performing can become near process' (2001a: 377). The example Grotowski gives of the *body of essence* is a photograph of George Ivanovich Gurdjieff in his old age, sitting on a bench in Paris.[27]

By perceiving essence during its osmosis, the Performer 'works the process: he develops the I-I' (ibid.: 378). The I-I referred to here is a feeling of being perceived or looked upon by another part of oneself, a part existing outside of time. The I-I is not a splitting of the psyche but something experienced as a totality: 'The second I is quasi virtual; it is not—in you—the look of the others, nor any judgment; it's like an immobile look: a silent presence, like the sun which illuminates the things—and that's all' (ibid.). The experience of I-I can be accomplished in the context of a still presence, when the ordinary habitual relationship of activity and receptivity is reversed: 'To be passive in action and active in seeing. [. . .] Passive: to be receptive. Active: to be present' (ibid.).

In his 2004 interview with Kris Salata, Richards describes the linking of the internal process with essence. In his discussion of this process there is, yet again, a connection made to memory. Richards gives an example of the nature of this work in relation to his long-time collaborator Biagini:

> It's as if all levels of your being have now entered into a deep interconnecting with the other person. That's when the highway is open. Then, maybe there's a specific remembering that takes place as a kind of a doorway, or maybe the remembering is of the doorway itself, and suddenly something starts to appear that is not you, not your partner, but a third something, like a gentle wind, a substance (2008: 130).

FIG. 11: Grotowski's example of *body of essence*: Gurdjieff on a bench in Paris (1948).

Remembering, as it is described here, becomes a mode of accessing essence. It is the active process of remembering that has the potential of acting as a doorway unto essence: 'Certain memories can be deep, precious beyond explanation, doorways, because they may be a potential passage towards a certain special aspect of inner life' (ibid.).

The process of active remembering is the tool—or vehicle—through which essence can be touched, while the experience of essence is framed or figured as memory or a special kind of remembering. Richards portrays the experience of this special kind of remembering as a doorway to a third presence. This other or third presence, Richards explains, can also be perceived as the sensation of being seen: 'Something is seeing. You're remembering this presence and now it's there with you. And it is like being seen by that which you are remembering' (ibid.: 132). This sensation of being seen is reminiscent of Grotowski's discussion of the I-I relationship cited earlier, which involves the reawakening of the part inside of us that 'looks on'. Richards' description points to a complex—if not mysterious—reciprocal relationship between the one who is remembering and that which is remembered. It is as if in the process of active remembering, one perceives oneself as an object of remembering. The doer is at one and the same time the agent and object of remembering.

The nature of the work on memory may present many dangers for the doer. For instance, how does one begin to distinguish a real process of rediscovery from the mind's—to borrow Grotowski's term—confabulation? Richards describes the process of determining whether the doer is on the right track as a continuous practice of verification vis-à-vis the work leader:

> The crux of the work on Art as vehicle, daily, is going back to the work on songs and seeing where it's a confabulation. Even today, we were working and someone was singing, and I just had to stop the work and say, 'That's not it. Listen, that's not it. Now, the process is being substituted.' There's really a subtle thread, a kind of opening of an inner channel, or there is not. And if not, we need to analyze and look for the problem, we need to understand or just solve the problem. After we had talked, the person sang again and there it was, this incredibly subtle and potent presence. It seems like a mystery. Well, there is something mysterious about it, but it's actually simple and real work. The doer has a tightrope to walk on. It might take the person years, which is normal, to be able to clearly sense the difference between a truly living process and one that has become an echo of yesterday, or a series of 'symptoms'.
>
> In the *Heart of Practice*, I write about what Grotowski called 'symptoms'. There's the danger that the real process is substituted by symptoms, which is in fact generally a natural moment of crisis in someone's development. The person discovers something through work on a song, and then, when they try to relive that experience, they can't. It seems lost and sometimes just the symptoms of the process remain. From the outside it might even look as if it's happening, but someone with experience knows that it's not really happening (2009).

With time the apprentice begins to develop her own inner sense of discernment of what she is experiencing. Richards describes the beginning stages of this type of navigation:

> And what does the leader listen to? He's listening to experience, to a know-how that has developed over years of work. If, in fact, some kind

of process is unfolding inside of the person in front of you, something inside of you can follow it, react to it. There is a specific kind of listening that a leader in this work needs to awaken that exists between what is being perceived and a specific part of oneself. If this kind of listening takes place, perception can be evident, direct. It's like to follow the person as if you are two birds flying together. Even though you're not doing, there is a part in you that's present, a part that is in a kind of quiet expectation, a calm desire, there is as if an inner thread that is waiting to be touched; that part listens and responds.

It's as if each of us has a kind of plug that's waiting to be plugged in. And if you have been plugged in and plugged out and plugged in again and again—you start to know the difference. You start to have a sense of when electricity is present and when it's not. And when it's not present, it's just evident. It might not be evident to everyone, but it's evident to someone who has taken the time and really practised. Knowledge is made of up time and dedication (ibid.).

The process of verification described by Richards is not unlike the traditional practices of transmission present in many cultures, and is the outgrowth and continuation of the work conducted by master teachers such as Robart within the Objective Drama program and other phases of research. It is to this form of oral and embodied transmission that I will return in Chapter 4.

Conclusion

While Grotowski approached work with memory—which in his practice necessarily implied body-memory—in a variety of ways, memory functioned, at least in part, as a mode of inquiry, an instrument of rediscovery of essence. The return to essence in Grotowski's work, particularly in its latter phases, is figured in testimonies of the work as an experience of remembering taking place in the present moment while inextricably linked to the past. Grotowski writes: 'Is essence the hidden background of the memory? I don't know at all. When I work near essence, I have the impression that memory actualizes. When essence is activated, it is as if strong potentialities are activated. The reminiscence is perhaps one of these potentialities' (2001a: 379). Grotowski's use of the word 'reminiscence' in this context does not imply the more common contemporary usage, which is often suggestive of a process of casual mental remembering. The process of recollecting or recovering still contained in the modern definition of reminiscence seems better aligned with Grotowski's understanding and practice of active remembering discussed in this chapter. Grotowski's praxis associated with memory as well as his choice of terminology evokes Aristotle's notion of reminiscence, expounded in *De memoria et reminiscentia*, and understood as the recollection or recovery of knowledge or sensation (see Yates 1966: 33).

Memory, for Grotowski, marks the return to essence: the rediscovery of forgotten potentialities, the surpassing and realization of the self, the consequence of which is what he called in the early phases of research a state of transparency and luminosity and later referred to as the body of essence. This is achieved not through conscious manipulation but through a submission, a letting go, the cessation of struggle. This process involves a line of inquiry imagined as a return to one's ancestral past, but is fundamentally premised on the belief that in each individual's most intimate, precultural being is encoded all that came before: 'It's you, unrepeatable, singular, you in the totality of your nature; you carnal, you stripped bare. And at once also: it's you the embodiment of all others, all beings, all of history' (Grotowski 1979b: 135).

Notes

1 Around the time of transition to the Art as vehicle phase of research, Grotowski's terminology shifted from 'actor' to 'doer' to designate 'the artists who do'. In Richards' personal terminology the doer is one who works on the 'process of energy transformation in performing with and around these ancient vibratory songs' (2008: 9). I will discuss this work in more detail in Chapter 4.

2 In a series of lectures given in 1997 at the Collège de France entitled 'La Lingée organique au théâtre et dans le rituel', Grotowski showed fragments of Maya Deren's film *Divine Horsemen: The Living Gods of Haiti* (1953) as an example of these ritual structures and of what he has called the 'organic line'. Borrowing Stanislavsky's term, Grotowski defined 'organicity' as the flow of impulses that precedes and liberates small actions. The consequence of this flow of impulses is the visible fluidity and continuity of actions, which Grotowski contrasts to a staccato motion (1995b: 13). Stanislavsky's usage of 'organic actions' refers to actions that have their own logic and must be performed in a specific order (Benedetti 1998: 153). While Grotowski's usage of the term originates with

Stanislavsky it transcends the quotidian social realm to which Stanislavsky's understanding of 'organicity' was confined. I will return to the discussion of Grotowski's understanding of organicity later in this book.

3   While references to Grotowski's travels are many, they are dispersed throughout the literature on Grotowski. At present no study on Grotowski contains a comprehensive description or even a listing of all of his journeys. However, for the most thorough discussion of Grotowski's journeys in the Western hemisphere, see Kermit Dunkelberg (2008).

4   All quotes from this text are my translation.

5   I intentionally omit the term actor 'training' here because Grotowski devotes a large part of this talk to explaining and demonstrating the ways in which conventionally understood actor 'training' is not helpful but, in fact, blocks the actor's creativity. Grotowski's choice of the word 'Exercises' for the title was strategic and intended to disrupt the popular notion of the actor's preparatory work. This English equivalent for the Polish word *ćwiczenie* is only approximate. The Polish word contains within it a notion of practice. For instance, the verbal form *ćwiczyć* is closest to the English verb 'to practise'.

6   In Grotowski's terminology, an 'authentic reaction' would have implied a direct, unmediated and sincere reaction to stimuli, one that might be contrasted with a superficial, cliched, affected, contrived or mechanical response.

7   Grotowski differentiates activities and actions along the same lines as Stanislavsky's method of physical actions. While activities such as drinking a glass of water or sweeping the floor do not constitute actions in themselves, they may become physical actions if the actor performs them with conscious awareness and intent. Physical actions are what an actor undertakes to solve a problem or accomplish something. Grotowski uses the example of drinking a glass of water as an activity that if performed with the intent of stalling, for instance, because one is searching for an answer to a difficult question, may be transformed into a physical action (Richards 1995: 31).

8   Because, to my knowledge, there is no English publication of this text, I quote at length here.

9   From 1986 to 2000 Carla Pollastrelli was an executive of the Workcenter of Jerzy Grotowski. She has edited and translated numerous Grotowski texts from Polish into Italian. She is currently the co-director of the Fondazione Pontedera Teatro.

10 While Grotowski used gender-neutral terms when speaking and writing in Polish, his preference was to utilize the masculine pronoun in English translations of his talks and texts. However, he pointed to the problem of translation by often placing the Polish original in parentheses following an English term he did not feel adequately reflected the original. While acknowledging Grotowski's preference, I have chosen to diverge from his usage and employ gender-neutral terms as well as alternate between masculine and feminine pronouns throughout this text.

11 While the moments revivified by Cieślak are those of an early experience of making love, Grotowski's subsequent characterization of this experience is not as that of sexuality but rather as a liminal state between prayer and sensuality. Grotowski's references to this example abound, and can be found, among others, in Grotowski (1992), Ahrne (1993) and Grotowski (1995a).

12 At a public talk given at New York University on 23 April 2009, Mieczysław Janowski, who played the role of the Muley in *The Constant Prince*, demonstrated that performance scores developed by the other actors were based on improvisations of highly stylized cafe scenes and contrasted greatly with Cieślak's score, which was developed separately with Grotowski over a period of many months. Janowski recalls the profound difference in the quality of Cieślak's score and how he and the other actors had to work in order to bridge this qualitative difference once Grotowski began to integrate the various acting scores.

13 The original French transcript reads:

> Nous avons retrouvé—pas comme une reconstruction mais comme quelque chose de vivant—une manière de s'envoler. Nous avons cherché et retrouvé les plus petites actions, les impulsions de ces moments remémorisés. C'était comme si cet adolescent se remémorisait avec le corps la libération du poids du corps, comme s'il allait dans un territoire où il n'y a plus de poids, où il n'y a plus de souffrance. Mais tout cela a été fait par les impulsions et les actions, les plus petites actions physiques, réelles, de son souvenir, d'un événement remémorisé, qui était à nouveau retrouvé—pas reconstruit—pour s'envoler (Ahrne 1993: 5).

A modified translation of this quotation is available at Ahrne (2009: 224).

14 Tiga and Robart joined the Objective Drama research team as master teachers. Robart continued to work with Grotowski through the Art as vehicle phase until 1993.

15 Since all songs possess vibratory qualities, it is my inference that the naming of these particular songs rooted in the ancient ritual practices of the Afro-Caribbean tradition is meant to emphasize the complex vibratory patterns that conduct internal work or *perform on the body* of the doer.

16 While Grotowski differentiated the various qualities of energy, from the more dense energy to the more subtle, he did not intend to qualify these distinct energies in terms of good and bad. Higher and lower simply indicates the position of the energy in relation to the body.

17 Lisa Wolford changed her name to Lisa Wolford Wylam. In my citations I have used the name under which the publication appears. In referring to her outside quotations I have used Lisa Wolford Wylam.

18 Recognized as one of the first behavioural geneticists, Sir Francis Galton (1822–1911) convinced his cousin, Charles Darwin, that the principles of natural selection applied to behaviour as well as physical characteristics. The question within the contemporary field of behaviour genetics studies is no longer whether a trait is due to nature or nurture but, instead, the extent to which each of these factors and the interactions between them influence the development of a particular trait. Since the 1980s, there has been a proliferation of behaviour genetic studies exploring psychological development. These studies assess phenotypes involved in both normal and abnormal development. For further reading see Benjamin, Ebstein and Bellmaker (2002); Plomin et al. (2003); and Rutter and Silberg (2002).

19 The 'active gene-environment correlation' occurs when an individual possesses a heritable propensity to select environmental exposure.

20 In the terminology deployed by Grotowski starting in the Objective Drama phase of research, Action with a capital *a* denoted a precise performative structure—an opus. *Action* italicized was used to refer to the titles of various opuses within the work, such as *Main Action* (1985–86, Irvine, California), *Pool Action*, *Remembering Action* and *Downstairs Action* (1988–92 Pontedera, Italy) and *Action* (1994–2007, Pontedera, Italy).

21 The prevalent and systematic translation of the term *człowiek* as 'man' in English-language editions of Grotowski's writing has often been interpreted as Grotowski's masculinist imaginary of the performer. However, Grotowski's consistency in using nongendered language in his Polish writings and talks undermines this reading—at least on the level of linguistic analysis. It is neither the case that these misunderstandings have arisen through faulty translations. Some sources suggest that Grotowski's use of the English 'man' instead of what might be a more accurate equivalent of 'human being' is strategic, in that Grotowski was interested in creating an allusion to the language used in the King James version of the Bible.

22 It is difficult to find a graceful equivalent; the most literal translation might be expressed as 'being of discovery'.

23 While in the instance to which Richards refers the process might lead to a remembering or embodiment of his father that is distinct from the 'ancient corporality' described by Grotowski in the 'Performer', an analogous interrogatory process may be used to search for an 'ancient corporality'.

24 The apparent association of African warriors with an ancestral corporality, which has the implicit overtones of classifying the African body with primitivism or situating it at an earlier moment along some sort of temporal and developmental progression is undoubtedly very problematic. I will discuss Grotowski's complex relationship to transgenerational and intercultural transmission in Chapter 4.

25 I will discuss the nature of the evidentiary process and what constitutes evidence in this context in more depth in Chapter 2.

26 Kanze Zeami (1364–1444), also known as Zeami Motokiyo, was a Japanese actor, playwright and critic. In his theoretical works on the art of the Noh, Zeami writes extensively about his notion of *hana* (flower) in *Kadensho* (On transmitting the flower, 1400) and in *Shikadosho* (On the way of the highest flower, 1420). According to Zeami one can achieve the archetypal beauty of the flower by being true to one's own innate nature and the surrounding circumstances. The beauty attained in this manner changes with age and possesses an appearance suitable to the time and circumstance in which it appears. Zeami distinguishes between *makoto no hana* (genuine flower) and *jibun no hana* (temporary flower).

27 George Ivanovich Gurdjieff (1866?–1949) was a Greek-Armenian mystic and
   spiritual teacher. For Grotowski's discussion of his relationship to Gurdjieff
   see Grotowski (1997).

FIGURES 12 and 13: Brzezinka, around the time of paratheatrical events. Photograph by Andrzej Paluchiewicz.

CHAPTER 2

Czuwaj (*Be Vigilant*)
Vigilance and Witnessing in the Grotowski Work

From the very early stages of his work on the actor's craft, Grotowski betrayed a strong interest in creating a particular quality of being in the actor, characterized by heightened awareness or vigilance that, I will argue, in turn facilitated acts of witnessing. The processes that led to heightened awareness and vigilance were developed during the extended rehearsal process characteristic of the Laboratory Theatre's work. These processes were subsequently reactivated in productions, thereby functioning as evidence of discoveries made in the rehearsal process and bearing witness to the actor's vigilance and self-disarmament.

The practices of vigilance and witnessing explored in the final years of the Theatre of Productions phase were further developed and used in all subsequent phases of Grotowski's work. This work originated in specific concerns and took on various articulations, the precise nature of which is the subject of this chapter. A fairly early example of vigilance is the work referred to as *The Vigil* (*Czuwanie*), a paratheatrical project devised by Jacek Zmysłowski in the mid-1970s. In Poland, and indeed throughout Eastern Europe, there is a strong praxis of vigilance and ritual vigils, both collective and individual. These traditions held a special significance for Grotowski and Zmysłowski. Grotowski drew on the notion of vigilance in many of his talks and, along with Zmysłowski, devised paratheatrical work that was explicitly inspired by the Eastern European tradition of vigils.

Vigilance

From the beginnings of his research into acting, Grotowski explored heightened states of awareness within the actor. During the Theatre of Productions, this is apparent in the example of Grotowski's intense individual work with Cieślak. Work on reconstructing the precise bodily movement from a pivotal moment in the past required an extraordinary amount of attentiveness that led to heightened states of awareness on the part of both the actor and director.[1] However,

FIGURE 14: Andrzej Paluchiewicz, around the time of a paratheatrical event in Brzezinka (1974). Photograph by Andrzej Paluchiewicz.

beyond Grotowski's individual work with Cieślak, which was an exception as rehearsals were usually conducted with all of the actors present, Grotowski required tremendous attention, concentration and awareness not only on the part of the actor with whom he happened to be working but also from the other actors observing the process. Working in this manner at times required actors who were not actively engaged in the work to observe with the utmost attention for four or five hours at a time (Janowski 2010). Moreover, the use of techniques of vigilance—such as the observance of silence—deployed later in the paratheatrical research were already evidenced during the Theatre of Productions phase through Grotowski's imposition of a one-hour period of silence before performances. This practice allowed the actors to transition from the distractions of their daily lives into the nonquotidian space of the performance, which required a higher level of attention (ibid.).

In the beginning of the 1970s Grotowski, along with certain members of the Laboratory Theatre, gradually joined by new, younger members, embarked on the phase of research that became known as Active Culture. This 10-year post-theatrical phase of research, alternately called Paratheatre or Theatre of Participation (1969–78), was characterized by the dissolution of the conventional separation of actors from the audience. What Grotowski and his team explored was a new and total kind of audience participation. This move is clearly a development of Grotowski's earlier attempts to unsettle the actor-audience divide.[2] This process can be traced as a gradual progression back through *Apocalypsis cum Figuris*, often retrospectively seen as a transitional piece, to *Kordian*[3] and other productions.

During the paratheatrical period, an even greater opening occurred, in which experienced work leaders[4] created conditions for the active participation of others within paratheatrical events. Theatre of Participation events varied widely in their location, duration, structure and themes. The connective thread binding the various paratheatrical events was the attempt to rediscover modes of being with oneself and others that would depart from ordinary everyday encounters typified by clichéd behaviour, hiding behind social masks and moving within routinized and formalized structures of interaction. The paratheatrical phase retained Grotowski's pursuit of an authentic meeting formulated during the Theatre of Productions but altered the methodology of research to expand the possibilities for a more active participation on the part of the group heretofore known as the spectators.[5]

During this post-theatrical period, longtime members of the Laboratory Theatre—and younger members who joined the team successively—developed their own particular interests and research by way of devising and leading paratheatrical projects. In the 1970s the team members of the Institute of the Actor–Laboratory Theatre consisted of Elisabeth Albahaca, Rena Mirecka, Ryszard Cieślak, Zbigniew Cynkutis, Antoni Jahołkowski, Zygmunt Molik, Andrzej Paluchiewicz, Stanisław Ścierski and Zbigniew (Teo) Spychalski. They were joined by the 'young group': Irena Rycyk, Wiesław Hoszowski, Zbigniew Kozłowski, and Aleksander Lidtke (1970–71); Teresa Nawrot, Jerzy Bogajewicz, and Włodzimierz Staniewski (1972); and Jacek Zmysłowski (1973).

Meditations Aloud (1974), an early paratheatrical project led by Laboratory Theatre literary director Ludwik Flaszen, attempted to mine the possibilities of the spoken word against the limitations of ordinary verbal communication. Another paratheatrical project that became associated with Cieślak, *Special Project* (1973–76), was an attempt at a 'radical departure from conventions, the quotidian, games, impure or mercenary intentions, mutual fear and conceal-ment' (Grotowski 1975: 26). In the words of Grotowski, these experiments attempted 'to liberate in the participant, through the word, a process of recog-nition of one's own motivations' (ibid.: 24–5).

Special Project was paradigmatic of other paratheatrical events, in that its goal was: 'Meeting. Conceived as an inter-human encounter, where man would be himself ('as-he-is'), regain the unity (fullness) of his being, become creative and spontaneous in relation to others, rejecting masks, giving up pretence, the means of defense and attack, required of him by the nature of everyday reality' (Burzyński and Osiński 1979: 127). *Special Project* consisted of two compo-nents: one based on group work and the other on individual work. It was the former that became associated with the name of Cieślak. While the disparate paratheatrical projects became connected to individual names, it is important to stress that the projects—even in the conceptual and preparatory stages of the work—were highly collaborative and collective. The projects were rarely 'in the care of' a single person, rather, the team of individuals mutually influ-enced one another as they traded various experiments.

FIGURE 15: Ryszard Cieślak in Brzezinka. Photograph by Andrzej Paluchiewicz.

The following is a chronology of the paratheatrical experiments: *Complex Research Program* (1972–74), which consequently became known as *Special Project* (1973–76); *Spotkania Robocze* (Workshop Meetings) (1974–75); *Acting Therapy* (1975–77); *Zdarzenie* (Event) (1975); *Twoja Pieśń* (Song of Myself) (1975–76); *Otwarcia—miasto Wrocław* (Opening—the City of Wrocław) (1976); *Night Vigil* (1976–77); *The Way* (1977–79); *Vigil* (1978–79); *The Mountain of Flame* (later: *The Mountain Project*) (1977); *Medytacje na głos* (Meditations Aloud) (1974–81); and *Tree of People* (1979–81).[6]

Grotowski conceived of the paratheatrical research led by individuals or teams and conducted under varying degrees of his supervision as a 'self-directed research organism' (1975: 27) that, while capable of accommodating varied interests and an array of activities dictated by the different needs of its members, was collective and collaborative at its core. He differentiated between the intentions of various paratheatrical events, which he roughly divided into two groups of experiences—in the double meaning of the Polish word *doświad-czenia* (experiences and experiments). This delineation of paratheatrical activity was based on its underlying premise and function. One category of events, formally called 'laboratories', was more overtly utilitarian—albeit to use Grotowski's formulation 'in the highest meaning of the word' (ibid.: 26)—and had practical applicability to theatre. The main projects of this kind were the Laboratory of Theory and Analysis in a Group, Laboratory of Methodology of the Event and Laboratory of Acting Therapy (1975–77).

While Grotowski employed the terms 'vigil' and 'vigilance' in the context of various projects in the domain of Active Culture, here I will concentrate on the paratheatrical events with the word 'vigil' in the title (*Night Vigil* and *Vigil*), which make explicit the association to vigilance and the vigil. These events were conceptualized and carried out by Jacek Zmysłowski.

In 1973, at the age of 20, while still a student in the department of Polish Philology at the University of Warsaw, Zmysłowski[7] was invited[8] by Grotowski to take part in a meeting at the Laboratory Theatre's forest base near the village of Brzezinka, 46 kilometres north-east of Wrocław. This meeting, which lasted three days and three nights, was provisionally referred to as the first 'Holiday' and later became known as the first *Special Project*. On 2 January 1974 Zmysłowski joined the Laboratory Theatre as artistic co-creator, along with Grotowski, specializing in paratheatrical research. From then onwards until his final sickness and death in February 1982, Zmysłowski was very active in the Institute's paratheatrical activities. He took charge of sessions called *Ule* (*Beehives*),[9] which took place under the framework of the University of Research of the Theatre of Nations (1975).[10] Zmysłowski conducted one iteration of *Special Project* in Brzezinka and was co-leader, along with Cieślak, of the *Special Project* work sessions offered at the 1975 Venice Biennale. The following year he was responsible for the artistic realization of the *Mountain Project* and was supposed to lead the projected *Journey to the East*, a venture that was never realized.

Nocne Czuwanie (*Night Vigil*) is the name applied to a series of paratheatrical events that served as an introduction to the realization of 'Project Earth', a research project within the domain of Active Culture. *Night Vigils*, also led by Zmysłowski and his team, were open work sessions conducted on a regular basis—usually several times a month—in the years 1976 and 1977. These were held in the rooms of the Laboratory Theatre in Wrocław and consisted of a

FIGURE 16: Poster announcing The Mountain Project. Listed as distinct phases of this project are: Night Vigil, The Road, and Mountain of Flame. Poster design by Krzysztof Bednarski.

fluctuating number of participants ranging from a few to a few dozen. Most of the participants answered an open call announced in Polish newspapers and posters, inviting all those interested in active participation to join.

Night Vigil exemplified the stance of other paratheatrical events in that the organizers did not seek participants with certain skills or predispositions, but instead demanded only a readiness for active participation.[11] However, even this broadly-based criterion was dropped in later iterations of *Night Vigil* which became known simply as *The Vigil* (*Czuwanie*). While *Czuwanie* no longer demanded active participation on the part of the participant, it did not presuppose a division between participants and spectators. Rather, it allowed those participants not 'able to find the direct impulse of entering the action, not to remain an observer, not to be a spectator but rather to be—along with others— vigilant' (Laboratory Theatre n.d.: 1).[12]

An unsigned and undated Laboratory Theatre internal document describes the programme of *Czuwanie*:

> *The Vigil* is an attempt to go beyond routinized modes of being with others, an attempt to build a meeting among others—beyond demographic data about the other, beyond the narrative of oneself or one's affairs. It is a filling of space with one's own meaningful presence, mutually, together—through action, movement, sound and, at times, silence—so that almost every act, were it stillness, sound or silence is not inessential. *The Vigil* is a creative attempt, whose work is a *living process*, a becoming, a flow (ibid.).

The main thrust of the intentions behind *The Vigil*, as described above, is the attempt to initiate a process of heightened awareness within the participants beyond those experienced in everyday life. The striving for and potential attainment of these processes, with and among others, are in turn directed towards 'a meeting' with the other, a being together which constituted a recurring and central theme of not only the paratheatrical work but also the preceeding phases of Grotowski's research.

A reconstruction of what *The Vigil* might have actually been in practice is a daunting task given the dearth of archival material documenting this series of paratheatrical events. Beyond the single internal Laboratory Theatre document outlining the program of *The Vigil* cited above, the Grotowski Institute archive has scores of letters and postcards from interested participants. The length of inquiries varies widely from letters several pages long to postcards containing only a sentence or two. A reading of the letters of application underscores the open nature of admission to the events: in one letter a potential participant writes: 'I don't know if I am well suited for *The Vigil*, but I feel that I would like to try.' Another applicant admits: 'I am completely green, but I adore poetry and theatre.' Someone, who apparently took part in a previous paratheatrical project, likely the *Mountain of Flame* (*Mountain Project*), writes: 'The internal light which I seek, I found only on the mountain top. But it does not last long in this incessant clamour.'[13]

Participant testimonies obtained through interviews reveal that the experience of *The Vigil* had a powerful impression on them, but the passage of time has to a large extent eroded memories of the events. Participant narratives are impressionistic and often elude concrete description of what actually happened during *The Vigil*. Statements made by Katharina Seyferth, one of the international team of leaders of *The Vigil*, imply that her total absorption in the event itself—the way she threw herself into the work completely—actually *limits* her ability to remember specific details of the event. However, in comparison to other participants, *The Vigil* does remain more clearly imprinted in the memories of the international team of organizers responsible for leading this series of paratheatrical events, comprised of Rick Feder (USA), Sen Yamamoto (Japan), Katharina Seyferth (Germany), Zbigniew Kozłowski (Poland), François Kahn (France) and Jairo Cuesta–Gonzalez (Colombia). This team not only spent three or four months working together in preparation before opening the event to outside participants, but subsequently experienced *The Vigil* on numerous occasions.

Seyferth was invited by Zmysłowski to be part of the international team of leaders of *The Vigil* after participating in the *Mountain Project*. Seyferth had first become interested in the work of the Laboratory Theatre after participating in a workshop with Cieślak that took place in New York in 1977 organized by André Gregory. A German actress, Seyferth came to New York to study with Uta Hagen, but upon coming into contact with Cieślak and Grotowski, decided to pursue work with the Laboratory Theatre. It was already during the *Mountain Project*, a paratheatrical event in which she took part, that she experienced the work as a homecoming of sorts (Seyferth 2010). While the average duration of each individual's participation in the *Mountain Project* was about three days—the project lasted longer, but participants would rotate—Seyferth felt that she did not want to leave and was permitted to stay for an additional two weeks until the end of the action. Seyferth describes the invitation to continue working with Zmysłowski as being very informal. Beyond the fact that this new endeavour would be a longer project undertaken by an international group of leaders, not much was given in the way of description. Seyferth recalls that her experience of the *Mountain Project* made evident that they would be working on 'something similar' (ibid.).

According to Seyferth, the main task of the international team in the preparatory work on *The Vigil* was for each member to find their own 'individual movement or way of moving' (ibid.). The idea behind this embodied research was for each team member to actively look for and explore territory that was not previously known. It was an active search for something unknown conducted through nonhabitual work with the body. Seyferth describes this search: 'In some way we had to find something which was completely different from the everyday life that each person had or was used to. And even different from his usual perception of himself. [. . .] In some way we had to be ready each time. I mean to be ready continuously. We were waiting, in some way, to work' (ibid.). Seyferth's description makes evident the main thrust of *The Vigil*—the activation of a process in which one is continuously ready and waiting. This heightened attentiveness or readiness is intimately connected with the embodied exploration of the nonhabitual or unknown. The participant is continuously waiting, ready and vigilant in the face of the unknown.

The preparations for *The Vigil* took place mostly in Wrocław, however, the team would occasionally travel to Brzezinka where work was also conducted. Preparatory work did not follow a regular schedule. Team members would usually work for 12 to 14 hours a day for two, three or four days a week. Looking back, Seyferth speculates that this irregularity of work may have been dictated by Zmysłowski's health which was already in decline, although collaborators did not know about this at the time (ibid.). Seyferth also offers an alternative explanation for the irregularity of work schedules: 'It might have been a strategy to find a way towards something inside us, which we had to discover and which we didn't know. It was like a sort of research work which was leading to some unknown place. And because of this, maybe this was some sort of tactic, to proceed in an irregular way' (ibid.). While each iteration of *The Vigil* was unique due to the variety of participants taking part, Seyferth describes the overall structure or arch of the event, which was set in advance by the leading team:

> *The Vigil* had a very precise structure for us, the leading team. And what happened in some ways was in each time different because it depended on the people who were participating. [. . .]
>
> What was basically the process was that first Jacek [Zmysłowski] spoke to the people and we were already in the room. And we had— each one of us of the leading team—a place, a position. So Jacek would speak to the people and tell them a few things, like that they should not make too much noise, they should try to follow what is happening in the room, they should not become observers, they should not start to sing or to shout or throw themselves on the floor, etc., etc. And so, he was giving a sort of introductory talk to the people. And then he would place each person individually inside the room. And once everybody was inside, he would also come in and sit down. And so everybody was sitting in this room and it started like this.
>
> And then just with very little movement, of maybe just changing positions or putting the hands somewhere. In some way, our team was connected to Jacek, who was the leader and who was giving the tempo—maybe 'tempo' is the best way to say it—because it started very slowly. So we had, in some way, to create very simple and basic initial movement to get the people inside and, in some way, our task was to make the people move, to help them start, to enter the movement. We [the leading team] were like nine or ten people, and we had distance between us, but we were very attentive to what everybody was doing. And we were in some way starting a dialogue between us through the movement. Simple. Not expressing anything, just maybe through changing position, or standing up, or sitting down, or turning to the side, or turning the heads. So it was already like establishing some sort of net between the people who were also in between us.
>
> And then, very slowly, the thing would develop itself and things would become more energetic. Maybe walking or slowly going some- where. Movement became complete, embracing everybody, between us still. And then, depending always a lot on the people who were

inside because there were usually some people who had no problem to enter this, which was strange because it was not really talking. It was not really communication in the normal way. It was quiet, it was just moving in a way that the people were also not used to moving. It was very simple things. Extremely simple. So our task, in some way, was to help the people to make the first step to this movement, which became more and more like a current and a flow. So that's what we did and then usually from then on the things would usually take their own pace and so there was always some stronger phase. And there was one phase where there was a meeting, where we go towards the people directly and were meeting with them, in some way, doing some things, also simple, maybe just moving in the same rhythm or having some sort of simple dialogue through the movement. Then we went again toward the totality of each person in the room and the totality of the group and then in one moment the things would come to some sort of fullness and it was mostly in this moment that we slowly started to go toward the end. And the end was always quiet again. Going back again to the very soft movement, very quietly (ibid.).

Having taken part in numerous *Vigils*, Seyferth does not have distinct memories of each *Vigil*. However, what stands out most vividly in her mind are the times when something went wrong:

The most difficult thing was to always keep the people away from playing stupid games, or doing what they already knew, like yoga positions, or some kind of strange gymnastics. Or someone else would start to throw themselves on the floor. It's very strange, because people in that moment, they are somehow lost and they don't know what to do, they go back to some things they know already and what we wanted, or what Jacek also told them in the beginning, is that they should try just to discover something new and not to do the things that they knew already. So in some way, our task was also to try to keep them away from this habitual behaviour and to try and drag them into a different direction, towards the unknown (ibid.).

Zmysłowski himself roots the notion and practice of *czuwanie* within traditional Polish culture in a rare film documentation of the work entitled *The Vigil* (1981). The film, directed by Mercedes (Chiquita) Gregory and filmed by

Jill Godmilow, documents one of the iterations of *Czuwanie* that took place in November 1979 in Milan. In the film, Zmysłowski connects *czuwanie* with Slavic rituals that take place on the occasion of a birth or a death and offers his personal connotations of the practice of *czuwanie*, which to him implies: 'to be attentive in front of . . . to take care of . . . to be present before something' (in Godmilow 1981). Zmysłowski's emphasis is on that which happens *between people* in nonquotidian or extradaily contexts. His allusion to Slavic rites of vigilance connected to birth and death point to such extraordinary occasions during which groups of people become more attuned to one another and more attentive, or present, before 'something' other than that which is usually experienced in daily life.

The discussion in which Zmysłowski draws connections between the paratheatrical event of *Czuwanie* and the Polish practices of *czuwanie*, documented in the film *Vigil*, is a rare and important one. Because the work was nonverbal and verbal analyses of the work were discouraged, Zmysłowski and his international team were known for a reticence regarding any discussion of the work. The correlations drawn by Zmysłowski in the context of this film are significant in that they serve as apertures unto the interrelations of paratheatrical research and its cultural contexts and intercultural influences.

In the Polish tradition, *czuwanie* is considered an expression of a continuous readiness, a state of active waiting or anticipation closely aligned with Christian practice but extending beyond to folk, pre- and non-Christian rituals. In the tradition of Polish Catholicism, the vigil is a prominent practice of ritual anticipation or waiting for a holiday. This practice is undoubtedly rooted in the long-standing Christian religious observance of the vigil practised on the night, the eve and sometimes by extension the day before a religious festival or holy day. While Christian observances of the vigil were closely linked with various holy days of the Christian calendar, becoming more prominently associated with particular holidays depending on the historical and geographical context, the vigils held on the eve of Easter were considered particularly important in the early history of Christianity. In the fifth and sixth centuries, the vigil of Easter was deemed as the most appropriate time for other religious rituals such as baptism, the Eucharist and ordination (Zöckler 1949–50: 187). In the contemporary Polish practice of Catholicism, the most important vigil of the religious calendar takes place on Christmas Eve. It is unquestionably considered more important than Christmas Day itself, and figures as the most prominent holy day of Polish Catholicism. Christmas Eve vigil, commonly referred to as *wigilia*, like other rites of vigilance, is associated with fasting on the day preceding the holiday as well as a nighttime vigil culminating in a midnight mass.

Wigilia, like its English counterpart, 'vigil', comes from the Latin *vigilia* and connotes 'wakefulness', 'watchfulness' and 'watch'. It suggests a contravention of ordinary cycles of sleep through the keeping of a purposeful and active wakefulness during the night. The disruption of ordinary temporality or 'natural cycles' of routinized behaviour such as sleep, wakefulness and eating times was also a common feature of Zmysłowski's structuring of *The Vigil*.

Nocne czuwania (night vigils) are also associated with wakes in the Polish tradition. These are usually held in association with funerals and involve keeping watch over a corpse. Polish ethnologist Adam Fischer argues that night vigils were one of the pagan rituals against which the medieval Christian Church struggled as evidenced by the eighth-century *Indiculus Superstitionem et Paganorum* (Index of Pagan Superstitions) (1921: 206). The practices of 'excubiae [watching; keeping of a watch or vigil] funeris' involved spending time with the dead body accompanied by activities such as drinking, laughing, dancing and singing of 'carmina diabolica' (ibid.). Fischer links these rituals to Slavic traditions, citing the old Czech 'umrlčí večer' (eve of the dead) (ibid.). These practices rooted in pagan rituals are still prevalent in Polish customs associated with night vigils held for the dead, albeit in syncretic form, melding pagan practices with Catholic prayers and hymns.

The Polish practices associated with night vigils for the dead vary widely from region to region and range from solemn singing and prayer to merrymaking. Here, I will cite a brief description of one of the observances from the Kashubia region (Kaszuby):

> Among the Kashubians of Kartuzy County, on the last night before the funeral, neighbours and friends gather in the home of the deceased for the 'empty night' (*pusta noc*). Throughout the entire night they sit and sing church hymns, sustaining themselves with bread and coffee. If the deceased had an enemy with whom he was unable to reconcile before his death, the coming of his enemy to the 'empty night' stands in place of a reconciliation. [. . .]

In other regions of Kashubia we have similar data. The deceased is buried on the fourth night and during the preceding two, night guard is held near the corpse, a so-called 'empty night.' At nine in the evening the peasants gather in the house of mourning. The coffin with the deceased stands in the middle of the room with candles burning on each side. People sit or kneel on both sides of the body and recite a prayer for the dead. Around one in the morning, the guests are given coffee, bread, rolls, and in affluent houses even beer and vodka. At about three in the morning the people disperse. The last night vigil lasts until early morning (ibid.: 206–7).[14]

According to Jan Perszon, the source of the designation of the night vigil as *pusta noc* may be the old Polish meaning of the word *pusty* (empty), which signifies 'abandoned, deprived of power, forgotten' (1999: 197).[15] Perszon, who conducted ethnographic work among the Kashubians, describes various sources and meanings of night vigils given by his informants. Some situate the practices within ancient Christian traditions of prayer near the dead or claim that their behaviour is a direct imitation of the funeral rites accorded to Christ (ibid.: 201). Others, however, state that the function of the rituals associated with night vigils is to serve as 'protection' against the return of the spirit or, alternately, that it guards the deceased from becoming a zombie (*upiór*) (ibid.).

In the Kashubia region it is also customary to set up a provisional altar with a crucifix, a figure of the 'Mother of God' or other religious images or figurines decorated with flowers. There is special attention paid to ensure an empty space is left between the altar and the head of the deceased in order to give room for the soul to 'walk freely and stand at the head of the coffin, so it is not disturbed by those who come to pray' (ibid.: 193).

While Zmysłowski's conceptualization of the paratheatrical vigil may be rooted in traditional Polish practices that he is likely to have witnessed, the techniques that he proposed for the attainment of heightened awareness, readiness or vigilance—such as the prohibition of talking—clearly diverge from the practices described above. However, both Zmysłowski's *Vigil* and traditional Polish vigils provide loosely delineated structures that allow the participants to navigate the precarious entry into a liminal realm, considered spiritually dangerous in the latter. Both provide frameworks within which participants can begin to approach the unknown, to cite Seyferth's description of *The Vigil*.

As *Night Vigil*, the title of the early versions of *The Vigil*, suggests, Zmysłowski's *Czuwanie* aligned itself temporally with traditional practices of the night vigil. For instance, the only windows of the room in which *Nocne Czuwania* took place were painted black, obscuring the passage of time which could only potentially be marked by the sound of the bells coming from the nearby town hall located in the centre of town, a few steps from the edifice housing the Laboratory Theatre. Along similar lines, the duration of *Czuwania* was not set in advance. Without the imposition of temporal limitations, the guiding team, along with the participants, was able to intuitively feel when the event had exhausted itself and was coming to a close.

While *Czuwania* were inextricably positioned within the context of Polish and Eastern European practices associated with the vigil and vigilance, these practices have a wider transcultural grounding and resonance, often linked to a need for heightened practices of attention or guarding during times considered spiritually dangerous. Within the Jewish tradition, for instance, *vakhnakht* (watchnight, vigil), held on the night preceding circumcision, is intended to provide the male Jewish child with additional spiritual protection.[16] The Midnight Vigil, a practice of rising at midnight to mourn for the destruction of the Temple, introduced by the followers of Kabbalist Isaac Luria (1534–72), is a practice followed to this day in certain devout circles, particularly among Kabbalists and Hasidim. The Islamic practice of *tahajjud* or 'keeping vigil' involves the recitation of the Quran and prayers during the night and is considered particularly meritorious during certain periods, such as the holy month of Ramadan. According to the Islamic tradition, the night has secrets which are not revealed to those who sleep. The ascetic practice of *tapas* (Sanskrit for heat or ardour), carried out to achieve spiritual power or purification in the Hindu and Jain traditions, involves various austerities such as fasting, holding of difficult or painful bodily postures, breath control and vigils kept in the presence of fires or extreme cold.

Vigils connected to various traditions, and even within a single religion or tradition, vary in length and structure. However, there are certain features that bind these disparate practices together. The intention of the vigil is to raise the participants' level of attention, awareness or wakefulness. The event distinguishes itself from the quotidian. It often takes place on the eve of a holy day or in conjunction with a special event or occasion, such as the beginning or end of a life, or a rite of passage. It is an active preparation for something nondaily or extra-ordinary. The state of sustained attention, a characteristic of the vigil, is achieved in various ways depending on the particular instance; however, a broader consideration of the practices of vigilance does reveal certain commonalities. For instance, while some vigils in the Jewish, Christian and Islamic traditions require the use of speech, such as the recitation of prayers, this discourse is usually restricted to formalized speech and does not encompass casual verbal communication between participants. While formalized speech such as prayer and liturgical recitation constitutes part of night vigils of various traditions, this speech is situated within the context of the night, usually associated with silence and quietude. The calm and stillness of the night facilitates the possibility of redirecting one's attention to matters that fall outside the purview of worldly concerns. This implies the potential to free and consciously direct one's attention.

In Zmysłowski's elaboration of *The Vigil*, complete silence was observed and even nonverbal vocalizations were prohibited. This restriction placed upon ordinary modes of verbal communication created an opportunity for the participants to explore other means of contact. The elimination of verbal communication, and even sound, can be seen in the spirit of *via negativa* as a removal of that which is not absolutely necessary for a 'meeting' to take place. This simplification can be seen as an extension of traditional vigil rites insofar as the limitation of the use of verbal communication and sound has the potential to liberate attention and allow the participant to consciously redirect this awareness towards a specific end. This process of elimination undertaken by Zmysłowski during the paratheatrical phase is also evidenced by the elimination of elements such as props, which were frequently utilized in other paratheatrical activities such as the *Beehives*. Moreover, the chance encounter of working in an open space, such as the one undertaken in *The Road*, was also eliminated by situating *The Vigil* inside the Theatre Laboratory workspace and other interior spaces. Therefore, as Burzyński writes: 'Everything has been reduced to the simplest elements: you are, there are others, and there is some sort of space. The rest is to be found: in you, in others, in that space. Not as an intellectual task. But as *active search with one's whole self*' (Burzyński and Osiński 1979: 132–3; emphasis in original). According to Burzyński, the situation 'was *simplified* in order to *deepen* it' (ibid.: 132; emphasis in original). This simplification was seen as a kind of purification—a reduction to essence, which was the logical unfolding of the research Grotowski undertook in the Theatre of Productions phase.

Grotowski formulates his developing thought of the discovery of essence through the *via negativa*, or a process of reduction, in a 1975 interview:

> There is a point at which one discovers that it is possible to reduce the human being to the being that he is; not to his mask, not to his role, not to his game, not to his dodgings, not to his idea of himself, not to his clothes—but to himself. And more—this reduction to the human being is possible only through a being other than I.
>
> When there is a being together, when a human being is not afraid of anything—it is as if some knots are loosened, some shackles, as if everything was happiness; as if we were the pulsation of life itself. We are facing a flame, and the flame is also inside us (Bonarski 1979: 43).[17]

Grotowski's paratheatrical programme was perceived by some, including Burzyński, as something astounding: 'Astonishing, because in its verbal formulations it sounded almost mystical to some. Astonishing, because it did not fit either any real life experience, or cultural traditions that were known to us' (Burzyński and Osiński 1979: 108). While Burzyński sees a discontinuity between cultural tradition—*The Vigil* specifically, and paratheatrical activity more generally—Zmysłowski himself does situate *Czuwanie* within the line of traditional practices associated with vigilance. In the documentary *The Vigil*, Zmysłowski explains that *czuwanie* is an old word that has fallen out of popular contemporary usage in Poland. He alludes to vigilance practices at the time of birth, when women would gather around the mother to take care of her. He also mentions vigilance practised in association with death, a time during which people would practise vigilance or watch over the body of the departed. Zmysłowski's focus falls on that which happens *between* people on these special occasions when someone is coming into or leaving the world. His understanding of vigilance is closely tied to being attentive in front of something, taking care of something and being present in front of something. *The Vigil*, then, becomes an occasion during which these processes are not only possible but also intentionally sought after through the creation of certain circumstances by way of reducing or simplifying the conditions in which human interaction and interrelation takes place.

First-hand accounts of *The Vigil* and *Night Vigil* point to certain correlations between some of the underlying intentions and outcomes of traditional rites of vigilance. Jennifer Kumiega writes, 'If the *Night Vigil* can be seen as an awakening, the awakened are recognized, and the sleepers, untouched, sleep on' (2001: 242). Another participant who took part in the *Night Vigil* offers a similar description: '*Night Vigil* is a synonym for the awakening of the other pole of life, usually hidden in the night and sleep. Creating the possibility of contact with the unknown, it permits the participants to shake themselves free of everyday routines' (ibid., citing Kolankiewicz 1979). The *Night Vigil*, as defined above, aligns itself well with traditional practices of vigilance which allow the participant to encounter the unknown, with and in relation to an other, in an extradaily context. Kumiega observes a remarkable cohesion of consciousness and awareness that developed amongst the participants of paratheatrical events, given the relative lack of a code of behaviour or guiding instructions (2001: 244). Referring to her experience of paratheatrical events, which were located in interior spaces, Kumiega speaks of a containment that created a density of awareness and experience (ibid.).

Grotowski, speaking of the *Mountain of Flame* project more generally, deploys the terminology associated with vigilance to describe the intentions underpinning the project:

> Because our task, ours meaning the group who is vigilant [on the mountain], ought to be to recognize each newcomer and to find a natural, simple way of allowing him not to be a spectator. The mountain is a place in which when something *is happening* it is happening continuously—day and night. On the mountain there burns a flame like a column of fire, whether this consists of flammable material or in a completely different sense, a flame of something invincible, still continuously alive (living) in each newcomer, each day and at every hour changing, constantly adapting to that which people bring by the mere fact of their presence and take with them by departing.
>
> Over this flame we are vigilant. We are vigilant also, so the one who is tired can rest. So that the one who wishes may depart (1975: 24).[18]

In this context, vigilance takes on a more explicitly social and communal dimension as an activity that ensures that a quality is kept alive not through the continuous vigilance of a single individual or a group but by the rotation of people keeping watch. This understanding of vigilance as a collective watch-keeping in anticipation of a coming holy day reverberates with Grotowski's famous formulation of the programme Święto (Holiday), first articulated in two New York lectures given on 12 and 13 December 1970.

These lectures, the transcripts of which later became the basis of a seminal article entitled 'Holiday: The Day That Is Holy', published in TDR in June 1973, signalled a turning point and publicly marked the movement away from theatre in Grotowski's work that had already been well underway. One of the central issues with which Grotowski was preoccupied at this time involved the question of what is necessary and what is alive. Grotowski's most direct and simple response to this line of questioning is to propose two notions: that of adventure and meeting. Both are understood in a collective sense as actions discovered in tandem with others. Amidst this community of seekers—fellow travellers on the 'quest for what is the most essential in life' (1973: 117)—Grotowski poses the question: 'What is possible together? Holiday' (ibid.: 114).

While Grotowski refrains from explicitly defining Holiday, he gestures towards the meanings that this notion carries for him. Discussing a search that has to be carried out in accord with the character of the times, he alludes to the men who walked in the vicinity of Nazareth 2,000 years ago: 'Some men walked in the wilderness and searched for truth' (ibid.). This active search for meaning is, for Grotowski, inextricably tied to courage:

> If one does not possess that meaning, one lives in constant fear. One thinks that the fear is caused by external events, and no doubt it is they that release it but that something we cannot cope with flows from ourselves, it is our own weakness, and the weakness is the lack of meaning. This is why there is a direct connection between courage and meaning (ibid.).

The collective quality of the search for meaning in the face of fear is not only made explicit by Grotowski, but it is also underscored by the example he selects to illustrate his vision: Jesus and his disciples. Holiday is envisioned as a profoundly collaborative effort, inextricably bound to Grotowski's notion of meeting, in which 'togetherness' assumes a completely new dimension. As opposed to the understanding of the word 'together' as denoting conformism of an individual to a given group, a levelling or the giving in to the pressures of cliché, Grotowski is interested in togetherness as 'something like a second birth, real, overt, not furtive, not complacent about one's seclusion' (ibid.: 119). Of paramount importance in relation to this notion of 'together' is the other, or, to use Grotowski's term, 'brother', the one through whom one discovers oneself. Brother contains within him the 'likeness of God' and encompasses a brother-hood understood very broadly, including brother of earth, brother of the senses, brother of the sun, brother of touch, the Milky Way and grass (ibid.). Again, Grotowski ties this notion of brother and meeting to Holiday:

> Man as he is, whole, so that he would not hide himself; and who *lives* and that means—not everyone. Body and blood this is brother, that's where 'God' is, it is the bare foot and the naked skin, in which there is brother. This, too, is a holiday, to be in the holiday, to be the holiday. All this is inseparable from meeting: the real one, full, in which man does not lie with himself, and is in it whole. Where there is none of that fear, none of that shame of oneself which gives birth to the lie and hiding, and is its own grandfather because it is itself born of a lie and hiding. In this meeting, man does not refuse himself and does not impose himself. He lets himself be touched and does not push with his presence. He comes forward and is not afraid of somebody's eyes, whole. It is as if one spoke with one's self: you are, so I am. And also: I am being born so that you are born, so that you become. And also: do not be afraid, I am going with you (ibid.; emphasis in original).

Holiday, the day that is holy, it follows, is not only a time set apart from the ordinary, the routinized, the habitual; it is also, and perhaps more importantly, a way of being in the world. Grotowski's previous interest in meeting and disar-mament, dating back to the Theatre of Productions phase, is clearly discernable in this formulation of the notion of Holiday. Earlier practices of 'meeting' involved an encounter between the actor and the director, fellow actors, and the actor and audience, and the disarmament was enacted and embodied by the actor as epitomized by Cieślak's role in *The Constant Prince*. During Active Cul-ture, however, the parameters of the meeting were loosened. Therefore, the quest towards disarmament and, by extension, the rediscovery of essence, as well as 'the meeting' which had been part of Grotowski's research all along, no longer had to be contained within the theatrical context. While the initial stages of this research were made possible through the conditions permitted by working within an institutionalized structure subsidized by the state, this professional theatrical context was a shell that could be discarded given the right conditions. While Grotowski's interest and desire for disarmament, rediscovery of essence and meeting undoubtedly preceded his professional work within the theatrical domain, during the phase of paratheatrical research the importance of *again* marking these acts *as human and not professional* became evident.

Grotowski's question—the same question that elicited a response in the form of the ideas and practices formed around the notion of 'Holiday'—'What is possible together?'—reveals a deep resonance with Zmysłowski's focus in *The Vigil* on that which takes place *between people* during rites of vigilance. The centre of gravity in Zmysłowski's paratheatrical work associated with the vigil and practices of vigilance was the active attempt to rediscover human relationality in a nonquotidian context. The emphasis of *The Vigil* on that which takes place between people when their attention is directed in particular ways is the quintessence of Grotowski's discussion of 'meeting' in relation to Holiday:

> To cross the frontiers between you and me: to come forward to meet you, so that we do not get lost in the crowd—or among words, or in declarations, or among beautifully precise thoughts. For a start, if we work with each other—to touch you, to feel your touch, to look at you, to get rid of fear and shame into which your eyes drive me when I am accessible to them, whole. Not to hide, to be as I am. [. . .] To find a place where communion is possible. [. . .] It will rather be a meeting; not a confrontation, but—how shall I put it—common-holiday (ibid.: 133–4).

Finding a way of being in which it becomes possible not to feel shame before the eyes of an other, a shame that—according to Grotowski—invariably breeds lies, is at the crux of Grotowski's exploration articulated at this phase of research as a human need that leads to the active search for how to live without the shame of self. It is this that he considers the real proposition. In this quest there is no longer a distinction between artist and spectator: 'the artist does not exist; the only being that exists is man, who in meeting is there *earlier* than others' (ibid.: 135; emphasis in original).

While the theme of vigilance was most explicitly addressed in the work led by Zmysłowski, Grotowski's interest in heightened awareness continued to extend beyond Paratheatre into subsequent stages of research. In the Objective

Drama programme based and carried out at UC-Irvine, the work initiated by Zmysłowski in *The Vigil* influenced the development of a structure known as *Watching*. Even more explicitly linked to the Latin etymological roots of *vigilia*, the exercise *Watching* evolved from Grotowski's work with Jairo Cuesta, one of *The Vigil*'s team leaders. In his research at Irvine, Grotowski re-examined the strategies deployed by Zmysłowski in *Czuwanie*. He asked Cuesta to recall the ways in which Zmysłowski worked in order to elaborate a structure that would develop the quality of participants' attention in the work. Beside being an exercise based on *conjunctio-oppositorum*,[19] the juxtaposition of structure and spontaneity, '[w]*atching* also tests the participant's quality of attention. The primary objective is to watch, as the name suggests. You can't go to sleep. Wake up and watch. But watch actively, through movement' (Slowiak and Cuesta 2007: 130).

The idea of an active wakefulness, which continued to be developed in this phase of research, can be conceived as an active doing, an attentive watching through the movement of the body. Vigilance, or wakefulness, is also figured here not only as a doing, but as nondoing of something else, namely, sleeping.

Witnessing[20]

According to Grotowski, it is the 'true act' performed by the actor that transforms the spectator into a witness. The 'true' or 'total act' is understood as a stripping away of the layers of social masks: 'The act of the total unveiling of one's being becomes a gift of the self which borders on the transgression of barriers and love. I call this a total act. If the actor performs in such a way, he becomes a kind of provocation for the spectator' (Grotowski 1969: 99). The possible implications of this assertion are multitudinous. For one, in order for the spectator-as-witness to be possible or, more precisely, in order for the spectator status to be transformed into that of a witness, the actor must perform a 'true act'. In performance, an actor must act as witness or simply bear witness to her own personal discovery. That is to say that the actor's performance in front of an audience is an embodied act of evidence or testimony of a discovery that took place in the rehearsal process. The spectator-as-witness is possible only by virtue of the giving of testimony or witnessing undertaken by the actor.

Cieślak's performance in *The Constant Prince*, for instance, is seen as the embodiment of Grotowski's notions of an 'act of humility' and 'purification' in which the 'holy actor' offers or sacrifices himself through the realization of the

'total act'. In 1965, Polish theatre critic Józef Kelera, previously a self-admitted
sceptic of Grotowski's theories and work, writes of Cieślak's role in *The Constant
Prince*:

> A sort of psychic illumination emanates from the actor. I cannot find
> any other definition. In the culminating moments of the role, every-
> thing that is technique is as though illuminated from within, light, lit-
> erally imponderable. At any moment the actor will levitate. [. . .] He
> is in the state of grace. And all around him this 'cruel theatre' with its
> blasphemies and excesses is transformed into a theatre in a state of
> grace (1965: 73–4).

The actor in the context of this work bears witness to a discovery—an unveiling
initiated and realized in the rehearsal phase of research—by re-enacting it in
front of an audience. Grotowski virtually equates the act of revealing oneself
to that of 'giving of testimony' (1973: 121). Elsewhere, he states that when a fulfilment or realization takes place, it leads to testimony (1979b: 137). The accomplishment of the total act, when reenacted within a performance context,
constitutes evidence of a discovery or unveiling experienced by the actor and
transforms the actor-spectator dynamic into a relation between witnesses.

In 1997, shortly after his appointment as professor and first chair of theatre
anthropology at the Collège de France, Grotowski gave a series of nine lectures
entitled 'La lignée organique au théâtre et dans le rituel' (The organic line in
theatre and in ritual). In the third lecture, Grotowski spoke of the performance
of *The Constant Prince*, describing Cieślak's process as an act of self-sacrifice,
channelled by the most intimate associations of the actor (Magnat 2005).[21] In
the same context, Grotowski stated that one of the characteristic responses to
the work of the Laboratory Theatre of that time was that the spectators almost
never clapped at the end of the performances. Out of nearly 600 performances
of *The Constant Prince*, all of which were attended by Grotowski, he recalls that
clapping occurred only four or five times. In all of the instances when clapping
followed a performance, Grotowski felt that the performance was not successful
because the actors had 'played' but did not accomplish a total and true act
(ibid.). The more common reaction to performances of *The Constant Prince*
was the audience's long silence, crying and, at times, even screaming at the
end. In reference to the 'true act', Grotowski tells the story of having seen a film

of a Buddhist monk's self-immolation as a form of protest against the war in Vietnam:

> The film showed a group of monks sitting in three rows on either side of the monk who was about to be set on fire. The monks remained motionless, while one of them poured petroleum on the monk seated in the centre, subsequently lighting the fire and retreating to his seat. The remaining monks observed this act in complete silence. They exhibited no emotion. They were not spectators; their role was to bear witness. Only in the instant that the fire was lit was it possible to observe a subtle change in their manner of breathing—as if at once they all took a deep breath together (ibid.).

The goal of the Laboratory Theatre, Grotowski also remarks in this lecture, is to transform the spectator into witness through the realization of a 'true act' on the part of the actor. Grotowski's explicit statements about the role of the actor as enabling the transformation of the spectator into witness would seem to imply that the role of witness is potentially limited to the function of the spectator alone. However, it is the actor who 'gives testimony', thus, by extension, bearing witness or acting as witness to that which has been realized earlier, in the rehearsal process. Therefore, the function of witness cannot be restricted solely to the spectator. The decisive distinction between these two categories of witness is that the actor in the theatrical context is the one who actively bears witness or gives testimony, and in so doing creates the conditions in which the spectator has the potential of becoming a witness if a certain receptivity or vigilance is present.

The actor's act of self-revelation, fulfilment or realization is the testimony that enables a shift of the ontological status of the spectator. In later phases of research, Grotowski referred to the doer or Performer as *pontifex*, or bridge, which links the witness to the 'something' connected to what Grotowski attempts to evoke through phrases such as 'stream of life', 'presence', 'rhythm' and 'essence':

> Ritual is a time of great intensity; provoked intensity; life then becomes rhythm. *Performer* knows to link body impulses to song. (The stream of life should be articulated in forms.) The witnesses then enter into states of intensity because, so to say, they feel presence. And this is thanks to *Performer*, who is a bridge between the witness and this

something. In this sense, *Performer* is *pontifex*, maker of bridges (2001a: 377; emphasis in original).

In his introduction to the film documentation of *Akropolis*,[22] Peter Brook speaks of the significance of the witness in the Laboratory Theatre. He first establishes the essence of theatre as an encounter between two groups of people—the actor(s) and the audience. 'Theatre', Brook states, 'has to come to the boil in front of a pair of eyes. In front of a pair of eyes—and in Grotowski's language, the pair of eyes, the spectator, is the "witness"' (2009: 19). In Grotowski's theatre, Brook asserts, 'the actors commit extreme acts in front of witnesses' (ibid.: 20). He describes the example of a man who climbs a ledge on the 87th floor and threatens to jump as an extreme or atrocious act that makes 'no sense' unless there is a witness present. Brook contends that no communication, or necessity for communication, exists between the man who jumps and the potential witnesses. What is needed, according to Brook, is that the witness is present to perceive the act. Extrapolating from this example, Brook describes the role of witness within the Laboratory Theatre, and particularly *Akropolis*:

> The witnesses can watch dumbly, they can watch numbly, they can refuse, or in exceptional cases, they can find their way to a very great participation, but this is neither expected, offered, nor demanded. In all traditional theatre there is a basis of communication. Here, it is not about communication. If one doesn't understand this, one has no starting point with this very remarkable work. It is not about communication. It is about doing something or not doing something (ibid.: 20).

I would argue against Brook's contention that Grotowski's theatre is not about communication, and claim that *Akropolis* does not eschew communicative meaning, even meaning as narrowly defined as it is by Brook in this particular instance. However, what is key to recognize is Brook's insistence on the significance of 'doing something or not doing something', which he presumably juxtaposes between a theatre that narrates or describes and a theatre that brings into being. This association between witnessing and doing is also present in Grotowski's discussion of witnessing, albeit in an entirely different context. In an interview about Gurdjieff, Grotowski speaks of a particular way of 'bearing witness', which he understands to be 'an indication of "doing"' (1997: 104). Here Grotowski is delineating the difference between the communication of Gurdjieff's ideas and the 'bearing witness' to his embodied acts, or doings.

In keeping with the differentiation demarcated by Brook, Grotowski aligns witnessing with an indication of doing, of action—the embodiment of ideas or the praxis associated with a particular set of ideas—in contradistinction to the descriptive or verbal expression of the ideas themselves. In a theatrical context, witnessing as an indication of doing is embodied and enacted by the actor.

The 'doing' to which Brook refers in his introduction to *Akropolis* is associated with what he calls a 'bringing into being'. This for Brook is one of the distinguishing qualities of what he calls 'holy theatre', a kind of theatre which attempts to make visible that which is normally invisible. In the case of *Akropolis*, Brook argues, 'a quality of real evil comes into being' (2009: 21).

Akropolis premiered in Opole on 10 October 1962 and was subsequently revived in several different versions. The work transports the action of Stanisław Wyspiański's play bearing the same title from Wawel Hill to Auschwitz. The royal castle encircled by a moat and located on Wawel Hill in the centre of Kraków serves as the Polish equivalent of the Athenian Acropolis in Wyspiański's romantic drama. In Grotowski's production it is transposed to the extermination camp, which represents the graveyard of tradition and the necropolis of European civilization. Brook contends that in the production of *Akropolis* something of the reality of Auschwitz actually emerges:

> At certain moments in *Akropolis*, because a nameless horror was not described, was not referred to, was not something that once happened in a place called Auschwitz, it actually was brought into being. I think the particular value of *Akropolis* is what we want a work of art to be, it is real. The word 'real' has great sense: we want art to be real and not futile fantasy, dribblings of weak imagination. One wants something with a core reality (ibid.: 16).[23]

Here, again, Brook differentiates between descriptive and referential narrative communication and an action rooted in a reality, which having its own existence in the here and now, not only serves as an aperture to a past reality but brings this reality into being.

In *Akropolis*, the actors and spectators are distinguished conceptually as belonging to two disparate groups of beings: the spectators represent the living while the actors stand in for the dead. In a 1964 description of the production, Laboratory Theatre literary director Ludwik Flaszen writes:

> These are two separate and mutually impenetrable worlds. [. . .] These
> are the living and the dead. The physical proximity this time helps to
> confirm the separateness. The viewers [. . .] are provocatively ignored.
> The dead appear in the dreams of the living, strangely and incompre-
> hensibly. And, as in a nightmare, they surround the dreamers on all
> sides (2006: 64).

Flaszen points to a sharp division between those *bearing witness*, making manifest what Brook calls the 'pure evil' of the *Lager* (camp), and the spectators who
have the potential of inhabiting the ontological status of witness. Here again
the distinction is between those actively bringing into being through action
and those who have the potential of becoming witness.

What does it mean, precisely, for the spectator to assume the ontological
status of witness? The witness—as understood by Grotowski, Flaszen, Brook
and others in relation to the work of the Laboratory Theatre—is there to perceive what can variously be called the total or true act; self-revelation, realization or fulfilment; or the bringing into being of a reality, of the real. Brook's
discussion of the requirements of being a witness are rather loose and unde-
manding: 'The witnesses can watch dumbly, they can watch numbly, they can
refuse' (2009: 20). With the understanding that nothing is asked, expected or
offered by the Laboratory Theatre creative team, Brook does, however, leave
room for the potentiality of the spectator to find her way to 'a very great participation' (ibid.). What the ramifications of this 'great participation' may be is
left unexplored by Brook. Nonetheless, one can presume that beyond whatever
this quality of participation may entail, the presence of the witness, according
to Brook, is that which gives the event its meaning. The act, as in Brook's proposed example of the man plunging onto the pavement from the 87th floor, is
meaningless unless a witness is present. In this conceptualization of the function of witness, it is her presence that gives meaning to phenomena. Brook's
contention is easily undermined by even a cursory consideration of the possible
meanings that an action without a witness may hold. In the example of a man
plunging to his death, one must simply enlarge the frame and consider the possible meanings that this act might have had for the person taking his own life
or the people who learn about his action after its execution. Witnessing can
take place through mediated acts as well as witness acts that are mediated. What
is more, however, Brook's theory is further undermined if one considers the

last phase of Grotowski's research, Art as vehicle, the name of which Brook himself coined. The very essence of the work undertaken in the domain of Art as vehicle is premised on the notion on 'work-without-witness'. And judging by Brook's ruminations on that work, I presume that he does not find it without meaning.[24] The main fallacy in Brook's argument, as I see it, is the assumption that an act needs the direct and immediate presence of a witness, an 'eyewitness'. The reality that one can attach meaning to an act or a work of art that one has never eyewitnessed seems rather self-evident. However, this is not to say that the physical presence of a witness to an act does not have a special significance implying a particular ontological status.

Grotowski, on the other hand, in his discussion of the Buddhist monks who serve as witnesses to the act of contestational self-immolation, is attentive to and remarks upon the very subtle bodily changes of the witnesses. He observes the subtle change in the manner of breathing which took place in the monks the moment the fire was lit: 'Only in the instant that the fire was lit was it possible to observe a subtle change in their manner of breathing—as if at once they all took a deep breath together' (Magnat 2005: 90). In this discussion of the role of witness, it is the subtle movement of the body that is the sole external marker by which the witness can be discerned. The very nature of self-immolation performed by the monk as an act of contestation points to the etymological connection between the requisite presence of a witness and the very definition of 'contestation' as 'the action of calling or taking to witness, adjuration; solemn appeal or protest' (Oxford English Dictionary).

Whether witnessing the testimony of self-revelation or an act of contestation, the presence of the witness, in this context, gives meaning to acts. While the act of evidencing a discovery or fulfilment found in the rehearsal process that is later re-enacted in performance and acts of contestation may appear to reside on opposite sides of the spectrum, these two contrasting acts of testification come together in the figure of the Constant Prince performed by Cieślak. It is also in this role that the historical interrelation of witnessing and martyrdom can be discerned. Witnessing and martyrdom are inextricably entwined in both the Islamic and Christian traditions, the confrontation of which is depicted in Słowacki's version of Calderón de la Barca's *The Constant Prince*.

The Arabic term *shahid*, or witness, is tied to the signification of martyr. This twofold meaning of *shahid*, which binds witnessing to martyrdom, is also present in the etymology of the English word 'martyr', which can be traced back through the Latin *martyr* to the Greek *martis*, and signifies a witness, and more specifically evolved to designate believers who suffered death rather than compromise the faith. Some scholars argue that the shift in meaning of the Arabic term *shahid* from 'witness' to 'martyr' occurred under Christian influence alongside the Syriac *sahda* and the aforementioned Greek *martis* (Houtsma 1987). What is sometimes characterized as an ultimate extension of the attestation of faith at the core of witnessing (*shahadah*), martyrdom in the cause of Islam, is understood by some to be the supreme manner of affirming one's faith.

The confirmation of one's faith through the ultimate act of contestation—martyrdom—is also very much present in the Christian tradition as evidenced by the Constant Prince who, on the narrative level of the drama, bears witness to his faith by sacrificing his life. On another level, Cieślak's performance, as a 'true' or 'total' act of self-revelation, is a confirmation of his work of self-penetration and fulfilment discovered in the rehearsal process and as such qualifies as a form of the testification and evidence of which Grotowski speaks. Therefore, while the suffering and death of Crown Prince Fernando constitute acts of contestation (as well as the resistance to the surrender of the city of Ceuta along with its inhabitants as demanded by the Moors in exchange for the prince's freedom), on the level of Cieślak's action the performance is an attestation of the 'true act'.

While the number of witnesses to encounter the latter phases of Grotowski's work may have fluctuated, the status of witness remained essentially unchanged. With the exception of the paratheatrical period, to which a great number of active participants were invited—and during which the witness had an altogether different function—the role of witness endured fundamentally unaltered.

The Objective Drama programme and the Art as vehicle phase developed in Pontedera, Italy, saw a marked decrease in the number of people who were invited to witness the work. Moreover, in these last phases of research the work gradually moved away from the spectator as the intended and main recipient of the work: 'Action is not made with the intention to serve the witnesses' (Richards 2009). But in the instances during which witnesses were invited to view the work, the perception of their status and role had not undergone significant modification. The doer, by fulfilling something that in the Theatre of Productions phase might have been characterized as the 'total act', and that in the Art as vehicle phase would be described as an ascension of energy, creates the potentiality for the spectator to become witness. Alternatively, the doer makes it possible for a witness to—as Brook described when speaking of *Akropolis*—'find [one's] way to a very great participation' (ibid.).

When questioned in 2004 by Kris Salata about the changing function of witnesses in the Workcenter's activities, Richards replied: 'Our way of thinking about the role of witness has not really changed, but something is gradually transforming in time' (ibid.). His explication that follows seems to indicate that while '*Action* is not made with the intention to serve the witnesses' (ibid.), witnesses who are exposed to the work over a period of time begin to explore 'what takes place inside the opuses' (ibid.). The process that can potentially be experienced by the witness in Art as vehicle has a direct correlation to the nature of what takes place inside the doer. In the same way that the internal process of the doer in Art as vehicle has transformed from the internal work of a Laboratory Theatre actor, the potential experience of the witness in relation to the work has also shifted. In Art as vehicle, and more generally in art that is vertically encoded,[25] according to Richards, there exists for the witness a possibility of experiencing 'something like a subtle ascension' (ibid.). Using the example of certain ancient churches as vertically encoded works of art, Richards elucidates the potential effect that this type of art may have on the witness:

> Their form suggests an inner movement towards both above and below, a transformation of energy. [. . .] You can come into contact with this kind of artwork and as if lay your being on it. Laying your being on the work of art, you let the artwork realign it, let something inside you stand up, rise. [. . .] They can give life to an intuition. You are quiet for some moments; you feel the quality of the place penetrate you, something like a subtle ascension appears and you repose your perception very gently on the artwork, discovering that, if approached with a certain quality of attention, the artwork can actually favour receptivity (ibid.).

It is vertically encoded art and, by extension, work in the domain of Art as vehicle, which, by favouring receptivity, may point back to the distinction between spectator and witness, articulated much earlier by Grotowski. The witness in various phases of research is receptive and contains the potential for that 'great participation', which may also be what Grotowski was referring to when speaking about an inner movement that occurred between doers and witnesses of *Action*, by comparing it to a process of electromagnetic induction (ibid.). This analogy alludes to bringing about an electric or magnetic state in a body, for instance, by its mere proximity to an electrified or magnetized body and the potential relationship between the doer and a witness.

Beyond the momentary possibility of attunement or realignment of the internal state of the witness who is receptive to the doer in the process of energetic ascension, there exists a potential for the work to leave a more marked or enduring impression on the witness. Richards, speaking of the possible impact of vertically encoded art on the witness, states: 'A witness of such a performative process can become aware that what is happening in front of him can leave traces inside him' (ibid.).

Conclusion

Throughout various phases of his research, Grotowski exhibited a clear movement away from more conventional forms of theatrical spectatorship. This retreat from popular conceptualizations of the spectator is evident in his paratheatrical phase—among others—and is specifically related to the notion of vigilance. In *The Vigil*, there is an alternative proposition offered to the standard divide between actor and audience, active and passive: 'not to remain an observer, not to be a spectator but rather to be—along with others—vigilant' (Laboratory Theatre n.d.: 1). Vigilance is the very means by which the movement away from spectatorship has the potential to take place. Grotowski, again, gestures towards this in the following statement about paratheatrical work: 'Because our task, ours meaning the group who is vigilant [on the Mountain], ought to be to recognize each newcomer and to find a natural, simple way of allowing him not to be a spectator' (1975: 24). Vigilance is proposed as an alternative mode of being within an action in which an expanded receptivity may replace the conventional understanding of both the spectator as a passive receptor and the performer as the active agent of action. Vigilance in this context is seen as a heightened form of receptivity which is inherently nonpassive.

Moreover, it is vigilance as a quality of heightened attentiveness and awareness, both on the part of the actor and doer as well as the spectator, that leads to acts of testification and witnessing, and creates the space within which the status of witness may emerge.

Activating a process of enhanced awareness is the very means by which the performer can approach that which may be variously described as self-revelation, fulfilment and ascension of energy. In turn, these processes lead to acts of attestation, testimony and witnessing in front of witnesses—with the provision that the presence of those witnesses, at least in the domain of Art as vehicle, is not necessary to verify or give meaning to the processes experienced by the doer. The witness, if present, has the potential to find their way to 'a great participation'. Provided that a greater receptivity can be attained, 'something like a subtle ascension' may be accessed by a process which Grotowski conceived as a type of induction. By means of vigilance, it is a self-disarmament, realization, a rediscovery of essence, as discussed in the previous chapter, that is being evidenced by the performer and has the potential to be perceived by the witness.

Notes

1 A fuller treatment of this example will follow later in a section of this chapter which treats the notion of witnessing in Grotowski's work.

2 While the delineation of the influences of Grotowski's experimentation with the actor-audience relationship are not the subject of the present study, it is important to note that Grotowski's explorations did not happen in a vacuum. In Poland, Tadeusz Kantor experimented with the actor-audience relationship at least as early as 1943 with his underground production of *Return of Odysseus*, which in today's terminology would be considered 'environmental' or 'site-specific' theatre. Influences from beyond Poland were numerous. For instance, in 1968/69 Grotowski had seen Richard Schechner's production of *Dionysus in 69*. While much has been written about Grotowski's influence on North American theatre, an in-depth study of Grotowski's relationship to American counterculture movements is yet to be written. Grotowski himself briefly discusses his relationship to North American counterculture in Grotowski (1987a).

3 In *Kordian*, which premiered 13 February 1962, Grotowski set one scene from Juliusz Słowacki's great Polish Romantic drama in an insane asylum. The set, designed by Jerzy Gurawski, placed the audience members on metal bunk beds dispersed throughout the performance space. This spatial arrangement placed members of the audience at close proximity with the actors and, in effect, situated them in the position of 'patients'.

4 Experienced work leaders included actors of the Laboratory Theatre, such as Cieślak, and a younger generation of members who did not necessarily have experience as actors or performers. What distinguished the work leaders from other active participants of the paratheatrical events is that the former conceptualized and prepared the events in advance.

5 Later, Grotowski would critique this period of paratheatrical activity for reproducing the very clichés it intended to surpass (1987a).

6 For a more comprehensive description of this period of Grotowski's research as well as a description of each of these events, see Osiński and Burzyński (1979); Osiński (1986); Kumiega (1987); and Dunkelberg (2008).

7 Jacek Maria Zmysłowski was born on 3 May 1953 in Warsaw. He died on 4 February 1982 at the age of 28 at Memorial Sloane-Kettering Hospital in New York, where he was being treated for Hodgkin's disease.

8 At a talk given at New York University on 12 February 2009, Andrzej Paluchiewicz described how young people were 'recruited' for the paratheatrical work. This process was informal and entailed the older members of the theatre travelling to various cities within Poland and speaking casually to university students and others about their work. If common interests, which the work was to explore, were found, Laboratory actors would invite their interlocutors to take part in the paratheatrical work.

9 *Beehives* were loosely structured nightly work sessions usually conducted in the main room of the Laboratory Theatre in Wrocław. These events were open to all interested participants and while guests were sometimes invited to devise a *Beehive*, the activities were usually led by members of the Laboratory Theatre. In *My Dinner with André*, André Gregory offers the following description proposed by Grotowski: 'I [asked Grotowski] "Well, what *is* a beehive?" And he said, "Well, a beehive is, at eight o'clock a hundred strangers come into a room." And I said, "Yes?" And he said, "Yes, and then whatever happens is a beehive"' (Shawn and Gregory 1981: 27). For alternate descriptions of *Beehives* see Mennen (1975: 58–69) and Cashman (1979: 440–66).

10 The University of Research of the Theatre of Nations was held in Wrocław under the sponsorship of the Laboratory Theatre. Over 4,500 people participated in classes, seminars, workshops, performances, public meetings, films, demonstrations and paratheatrical events.

11 Active participation meant that one could not, for instance, sit passively and observe what others were doing and take notes. It tacitly implied that the participant was expected to join the activity initiated by the leaders. A member of the team of leaders of *The Vigil* describes the openness of these events: 'Everyone could participate. People from the street, like they could go to the theatre, they could come to *The Vigil*. Everybody was accepted' (Seyferth 2010).

12 All translations from this source are mine.

13 All quotes are taken from letters found in an unlabelled folder of loose correspondence at the Grotowski Institute Archive, Wrocław, Poland.

14 All translations from this source are mine.

15 All translations from this source are mine.

16 See, for instance, Goldmann (1926).

17 All translations from this source are mine.

18 All translations from this source are mine. While the biblical parallels of Moses and the burning bush may present themselves here, it is also hard to overlook the correlation between Grotowski's *Mountain of Flame* and the Indian mountain of Arunachala, which denotes 'Fire Mountain' in Sanskrit and where Grotowski requested to have his ashes scattered after his death.

19 *Conjunctio-oppositorum*, or the conjunction of opposites, is a term used by Grotowski as early as the Theatre of Productions phase to indicate the dialectical relationship between the rigour of a precise structure and spontaneity, organicity, or 'life' in the work of an actor.

20 Grotowski's production of *Akropolis* is a potent site for the consideration of traumatic witnessing. While it is widely known that set designer Józef Szajna (1922–2008) was a survivor of Auschwitz and Buchenwald, other Laboratory Theatre actors who participated in the production were also camp survivors. While a consideration of the relationship between traumatic and non-traumatic witnessing warrants a separate study, here I will limit my discussion to non-traumatic witnessing.

21 All translations from this source are mine. This article is based on notes that Virginie Magnat took during Grotowski's lectures at the Collège de France. They do not represent direct quotations of Grotowski himself.

22 The film documentation of *Akropolis* was shot between 27 October and 2 November 1968 in Twickenham Studios near London. The film was directed by James McTaggart

and produced by Lewis Freedman, Public Broadcast Laboratory. The film was first broadcast on New York Public Television, Channel 13, on 12 January 1969.

23 While I reject Brook's contention that something that once happened in a place called Auschwitz 'actually was brought into being' in *Akropolis*, I do allow for the possibility of the embodiment of 'a' nameless horror in the performance.

24 Brook writes, for instance, that he is 'absolutely convinced that there is a living, permanent relationship between research work without a public and the nourishment that this can give to public performance' (2009: 33).

25 For an extended discussion of Grotowski's views on verticality in art see Chapter 3.

Grotowski's Ladder

Making the Archaic Vertical Connection

Ritual Arts or Art as vehicle

In August 1986, Grotowski moved his research from UC Irvine to Pontedera, Italy, where, by invitation of Roberto Bacci and Carla Pollastrelli of the Centro per la Sperimentazione e la Ricerca Teatrale (currently Fondazione Pontedera Teatro), the Workcenter of Jerzy Grotowski was formed. Along with Pablo Jimenez, James Slowiak and Thomas Richards, three assistants from the Objective Drama programme, Grotowski began work in a former two-storey wine storage facility in Vallicelle near Pontedera. This move coincided with a new period of Grotowski's research, which proved to be the final phase.

In this final stage of work, Grotowski and his collaborators developed very precise performance scores which were deeply tied to archaic vertical structures present in various traditions, and whose function was to refine one's energies. More specifically, Grotowski deployed what he identified as ancient African and Afro-Caribbean songs and ritual movements that provided a physical and vocal structure along which more ephemeral work was constructed. This work involved the refinement of energies from the lower—more carnal and vital— to the more subtle. This more refined energy would then be reconnected to the vital and dense energy once again. In discussing this work Grotowski alludes to the powerful image of Jacob's ladder—a struggle to rise from the level of the purely physical to the psychophysical and, ultimately, the spiritual.

Initially known as Ritual Arts and later as Art as vehicle,[1] a term coined by Peter Brook, Grotowski defined this work in at least two ways. In one characterization, put forth in the essay 'From the Theatre Company to Art as Vehicle', which closes Richards' book *At Work with Grotowski on Physical Actions* (1995), Grotowski situates Art as vehicle along a chain of links comprised of the performing arts. Grotowski locates Art as vehicle at the opposite extremity of what he calls Art as presentation with which he associates his earlier work, the Theatre of Productions. The key distinction between the two extremities is that in Art as presentation the director creates the *mise en scène* or montage whose effect is discernable in the perception of the spectator. In the Art as vehicle, the seat of the montage is in the perception of the performers or doers, to use Grotowski's term of this period.

The second description of Art as vehicle offered by Grotowski in the same essay is more closely aligned with the work's initial classification as Ritual Arts. Here, Grotowski refers to the 'objectivity of ritual', a notion clearly carried over from the research undertaken under the rubric of Objective Drama. As in the work at Irvine, 'objectivity' for Grotowski refers to the precise and perceptible effects that certain ritual practices have on those who perform them regardless of their relationship to the tradition from which a given ritual originates.[2] 'Objective', in this context, designates a type of 'performative technique which has a determinable effect on the participant's state of energy, analogous to the objective impact of undegenerated ritual' (Wolford 1991: 165–6). In other words, Grotowski's work with ritual centred around an empirical exploration of the ways in which performative practices of certain traditions, such as Afro-Haitian song and movement, affected practitioners of diverse backgrounds. Working outside of the cultural context from which a given ritual originated, Grotowski investigated the observable and repeatable impact of these practices on the doers. Here, ritual practices were conceptualized as instruments that can not only be deployed as tools in the work on the self, but also have discernable and verifiable effects on the totality of the performer's being:

> When I speak of ritual, I am referring neither to a ceremony nor a celebration, and even less to an improvisation, with the participation of people from the outside. Nor do I speak of a synthesis of different ritual forms coming from different places. When I speak of ritual, I speak of its objectivity; this means that the elements of the Action are the instruments to work *on the body, the heart and the head of the doers* (Grotowski 1995a: 122; emphasis in original).

Grotowski speaks of ritual practices as tools that are either unknown or have been forgotten in the contemporary world. Conceiving his use of certain ritual practices put in the service of the work on the self as a 'reopening' of tradition, Grotowski designates these performative practices as instruments of 'verticality' (ibid.: 133). Tying together the two features of Art as vehicle, Grotowski explains: 'Concerning the persons directly involved in Art as vehicle, I don't think of them as "actors" but as "doers" (those who do), because their point of reference is not the spectator but the itinerary in verticality' (ibid.: 134). The link between doing and verticality is reminiscent of the connection between the designation of Performer as a man of knowledge (*człowiek pozna-nia*),[3] that is, one who 'has at his disposal *the doing*' (Grotowski 2001a: 376; emphasis in original). Having already defined knowledge as a 'matter of doing' (ibid.), Grotowski associates the concept and praxis of knowledge-as-doing with verticality.

The first mention of the notion of verticality in the essay 'From the Theatre Company to Art as Vehicle' is preceded by a discussion of what Grotowski identifies as 'horizontality', work whose centre of gravity is tied to the 'horizontal' plane (1995a: 121). He links horizontality 'with its vital forces, prevalently corporeal and instinctive' (ibid.) to the early phases of his research culminating in the Theatre of Sources. These stages of his research trajectory, while important in their own right, were nevertheless blocked on the horizontal plane as a result of the 'predominance of the vital element' that obstructed a movement above this level towards work situated along a vertical axis. It is in the research conducted during the Art as vehicle phase that Grotowski attempted for the first time to consciously and deliberately explain what he understood as the difference between the horizontality of his previous work and the verticality of the work he was proposing.

Grotowski shed light on what he meant by the vertical by using the image of what he called a 'primitive elevator':

> It's some kind of basket pulled by a cord, with which the doer lifts himself toward a more subtle energy, to descend *with this* to the instinctual body. This is the objectivity of the ritual. If Art as vehicle functions, this objectivity exits and the basket moves for those who do the *Action* (ibid.: 125; emphasis in original).

In this fragment of the text Grotowski first introduces the idea of rising towards a more subtle energy and immediately accentuates the need to bring this subtle energy back to the dense and vital energy of the body, previously associated with horizontality or 'the living body in the living world' (ibid.: 121). Grotowski conceives of verticality in terms of various categories of energy and the upward and downward movement along this axis. This movement begins with the 'coarse', quotidian-level energy, grounded in the body and connected to life forces—instincts and sensuality—and moves through more subtle energies towards a 'higher connection' before descending once again to the heavy but organic energies of the 'density' of the body (in Grotowski ibid.: 125).

Grotowski is restrained in his discussion of verticality. After gesturing towards a process of ascension and descent along a vertical line, he states that saying more—in this context—would not be right. Before comparing his description of the work oriented along the vertical axis to Jacob's ladder, he remarks:

> The point is not to renounce part of our nature—all should retain its natural place: the body, the heart, the head, something that is 'under our feet' and something that is 'over our head'. All like a vertical line, and this verticality should be held taut between organicity and *the awareness*. *Awareness* means the consciousness which is not linked to language (the machine for thinking), but Presence (ibid.: 125; emphasis in original).

The image of a verticality held taut between organicity and awareness—an awareness understood as direct perception and nondiscursive consciousness—is Grotowski's most concise definition of the research conducted in Art as vehicle.

In discussing Art as vehicle, Grotowski very quickly established a relationship between this work and the performative traditions of the past, and specifically to what he calls the 'ancient Mysteries' (ibid.: 120). However, beyond correlating the montage-of-actions of the doer in both ancient mysteries and Art as vehicle, Grotowski does not elaborate the relationship between these performance practices separated in time by many centuries. Grotowski scholars also allude to this connection, but their treatment of this relationship is sparse. In her introductory essay to the *Grotowski Sourcebook* Lisa Wolford Wylam gestures to this association: '[Grotowski] (re)appropriated the means and structure of performance to serve an explicitly esoteric goal, establishing a type of performance practice that attempted to reconstitute certain elements associated with Orphic and Eleusinian Mysteries' (Wolford 2001: 14).

Osiński, citing Brook and Mircea Eliade, also positions Grotowski's research in the context of the Western esoteric tradition and the tradition of mysteries:

> Peter Brook said that from time immemorial there have been centers that are not unlike the one conducted by Grotowski at the present.

(They have been called, I would add, mysteries [misteria], centers for work on oneself, etc.) [. . .] This work is closely linked with ancient rituals and the 'art of performing' in the traditional, archaic sense. Analogies to the ancient mysteries are also clear. Grotowski's work might in fact be seen as part of the 'great mysteriosophical movement in the West, which at the beginning of our era embraced gnosticism, hermeticism, Greco-Egyptian alchemy, and the tradition of the mysteries' (2001a: 395, citing Eliade 1984: 217).

The connection between ancient mysteries and Grotowski's research, alluded to by Grotowski and reiterated by others, is not limited to his research conducted in the domain of Art as vehicle. In his talk on 4 May 2009 at New York University, Osiński presented material alluding to Grotowski's much earlier interest in the tradition of ancient mysteries.[4] Osiński cites Grotowski's discussion of the use of the term of 'secular mysteries' during the Theatre of Productions phase:

Grotowski said, 'Secular mysteries do not exist. Mysteries, by their very nature belong to the religious domain. In our programmatic texts we used the term secular mysteries, but this was a code. If we said, that we are practicing a theatre with a direct connection with religious experience, this would amount to suicide. We used many similarly camouflaged formulas. The times were such, perhaps they are still such (at least in the West), the use of the word 'religious' did not sound good. Just as the term 'mystical.' These were indecent terms in secular societies, and certainly such was the artistic community in Poland at the time. The practice of sacred art was simply ridiculed and it was necessary to find some kind of a paradox. With the People's Republic of Poland as our backdrop, we really appeared as a theatre which had religious experiences as its source. 'Secular,' in this case, could also mean nondominational, nonconfessional. Besides, the use of pseudonymic terms has many virtues' (Osiński 2009: 9–10).

What is significant here is that the phrase 'secular mysteries' has been rendered as 'secular sacrum' in the English version of *Towards a Poor Theatre*. Grotowski's authorization of the English translation of the phrase might indicate that the avoidance of the closest English equivalent of 'secular mysteries' was strategic. Whatever the intention behind this modification of terms in the English rendition, it is likely that this shift in terminology obscured the connection between Grotowski's early work vis-à-vis the tradition of ancient mysteries.

While the particular form of performance research conducted by Grotowski in the domain of Art as vehicle has clear precedents and can even be traced as a logical progression through various phases of his own work, any attempt at mapping the traditional sources from which he drew necessarily produces a much more complex picture of the work's genealogy. Of the connective thread within his own development, Grotowski writes:

> In appearance, and for some people in a scandalous or incomprehensible manner, I passed through contradictory periods; but in truth [. . .] the line is quite direct. I have always sought to prolong the investigation, but when one arrives at a certain point, in order to take a step forward, one must enlarge the field. The emphases shift [. . .]. Some historians speak of cuts in my itinerary, but I have more the impression of a thread which I have followed, like Ariadne's thread in the labyrinth, one sole thread. And I am still catching clusters of interests that I had also before doing theatre, as if everything must rejoin (Thibaudat 1995, cited in Wolford 2001: 6).

Thus, while the image of Grotowski's own itinerary can be figured as following a single thread, the source traditions from which he drew—where the thread is tied—form a more intricate design. While the sites of Grotowski's investigations can be roughly categorized as esoteric practices, and particularly those focused on techniques of the body, their historical, geographical and cultural contexts varied immensely.

From a chronological perspective of Grotowski's own life, there are two early inspirations which provided very potent currents permeating his entire life's work. These were Christian Gnosticism and South Asian (Indian) philosophy. The way in which both influences came into his life is not insignificant. Jill Godmilow's 1980 film, *With Jerzy Grotowski, Nienadówka*, which traces Grotowski's return to the village of Nienadówka where he, his mother Emilia Grotowska and his older brother Kazimierz lived during the Nazi occupation of Poland (1939–45), is merely one of the documents recounting Grotowski's initial encounter with these two traditions. Grotowski's continual return to and retelling of these encounters in many other contexts points not only to the importance of the entry of these two influences into his early life, but perhaps more importantly, to the significance of the circumstances in which contact with the two traditions was made.[5]

In the Godmilow film, Grotowski recalls a time when his mother set out on foot to make a journey from Nienadówka to the city in search of books, which she considered nourishment. She brought back two: *The Life of Jesus* (*Vie de Jésus*) (1863)[6] by Ernest Renan and *A Search in Secret India* (1934) by Paul Brunton.[7]

> My first reaction to Brunton's book was a fever. Then I started to write out the conversations Ramana had with his visitors. I discovered then, that I am not as crazy as I initially thought. I discovered that some-where in the world people are conscious of certain potentialities. This brought me much relief, and at the same time created some conflicts with my Catholicism (Grotowski 1987b: 103–4).[8]

The reading of Brunton's work initiated Grotowski's lifelong interest in the philosophies and practices associated with the Indian tradition. He cultivated this interest throughout his life as evidenced by the pursuit of this field along-side his theatre studies, both on his own and in consultation with specialists,[9] the lectures he conducted on 'Oriental philosophy'[10] as well as his trips to Central Asia, China and, recurrently, India. In later phases of his work and dur-ing the field research conducted in India, Grotowski's focus included the inves-tigation of yogic practices. However, these practices did not constitute the bodily repertoire on which he drew during his work in Art as vehicle.[11] These earlier practices represent important points of reference for Grotowski and serve as precise analogies to the work undertaken during the latter phases of his research. For instance, Grotowski relates mantra to his work with Afro-Haitian songs:

> The traditional song, insofar as it is an instrument of verticality, is comparable to mantra in Hindu or Buddhist culture. The mantra is a sonic form, very elaborated, which englobes the position of the body and the breathing, and which makes appear a determined vibration in a tempo-rhythm so precise that it influences the tempo-rhythm of the mind (1995a: 127).

While the philosophies and bodily practices associated with Indian traditions did not constitute the performative elements on which Grotowski drew most directly in Art as vehicle, his lifelong interest and intimate knowledge of these traditions were a formidable intellectual and practical reservoir which, while not always visible, informed his later work.

On the surface, it may appear as if the other book procured by his mother, Renan's *The Life of Jesus*, might be well aligned with Grotowski's Catholic upbringing. However, as Grotowski himself points out, Renan's work was forbidden by the Church. Despite this ban, Grotowski's mother, who was 'practicing the most ecumenical Catholicism', had an independent opinion of Renan's work and 'considered it an extremely important story about Jesus, and often repeated that for her it was the "fifth Gospel"' (Grotowski 2001b: 253). Not only did the effort exerted by Grotowski's mother in obtaining these two volumes influence the import that they had in Grotowski's life, but the illicit status of Renan's book undoubtedly shaped Grotowski's reception of the work.[12] The clandestine and unauthorized nature of Grotowski's encounter with the narratives of Jesus' life, also in the case of the canonical Gospels, created an atmosphere of reception that was extraordinary. Grotowski recalls his first encounter with the Gospels:

> In the time when I was living among peasants, the Church forbade reading the Gospels alone. The presence and interpretation of the priest was obligatory. Because I was asking to read the Gospels myself, I clashed with the old Catholic priest in the village school. He refused, of course. But his young assistant priest, in secret, gave me the Gospels, asking that his boss should know nothing about this, and that I should read it in conspiracy. In my pocket I carried this little book with its soft brown cover. I arrived to the farm where I was living. I put the ladder to the loft, which was above the little wood shed for pigs, I locked myself inside and I was reading. From above, I was listening to the grunting of the pigs. The light arrived through little holes in the thin wood wall. [. . .] Through these holes I had seen a very little hill with a couple of trees and that became for me the image of Golgotha. All topography of the village became for me the topography of the Gospel story (2001b: 253–4).

This covert reading of the Gospels within a soundscape permeated by grunting swine, which Grotowski imitates flawlessly in the film of *Nienadówka*, produced for the young Grotowski a very intimate relation to the text and Jesus.

Grotowski's confrontation with the Christian tradition and his working through of certain motifs central to Christian thought is clearly evident in such productions as *The Constant Prince* or *Apocalypsis*. However, the Christian Gnostic strain in Grotowski's work arises from encounters later in his life. For instance, the Gospel of Thomas came to constitute the core textual material for *Action*.

The Coptic papyrus manuscript of the Gospel of Thomas, alternately referred to as the Gospel According to Thomas, was discovered in December of 1945 near Nag Hammadi, Egypt and, along with 50 other documents, constitutes the Nag Hammadi archive. The document is attributed to the apostle Thomas but believed by scholars to be authored by someone else. The text begins: 'These are the hidden words that the living Jesus spoke, and that Didymos Judas Thomas wrote down. And He said: "Whoever finds the meaning of these words will not taste death"' thereby inscribing Thomas as the archivist of Jesus' words within the logic of the text itself (Patterson, Robinson and Bethge 1998). Like Emilia Grotowska's designation of Renan's *The Life of Jesus* as the fifth gospel, the Gospel of Thomas is a noncanonical gospel, unauthorized by the Church. However, it contrasts with Renan's work in that it is not a narrative of the life of Jesus but instead consists of 144 *logia*, or wisdom sayings, attributed to Jesus. These include sayings such as 'Jesus said, "Show me the stone which the builders have rejected. That one is the cornerstone" (66)' or the more enigmatic: 'Jesus said, "Become passers-by" (42)' (Lambdin 1990). The Gospel of Thomas diverges from the canonical gospels in a number of ways. Most notably, it always presents Jesus in his human and nondivine capacity and refers to female apostles, listing Mary (presumably Mary Magdalene) and Salome among Jesus' disciples.

While numerous translations of the Gospel of Thomas exist, Grotowski along with Mario Biagini worked on a new translation of the text from Coptic to be used in *Action*. The significance of the textual aspect of the work is evidenced, for instance, by the fact that Grotowski asked Biagini to learn Coptic expressly for the purpose of working on the translation of this text.

The rendition of the Gospel of Thomas used in *Action* is a literal, word-for-word translation which follows the original syntax. Although some scholars might find the practice of a 'word-for-word' rendition dubious with regard to translation, Grotowski was interested in apprehending, if possible, the mystic force of the original constructions even if these did not translate into a wholly meaningful modern language. The Workcenter translation of the excerpt of the Gospel of Thomas, uttered or sung in English alternately by Biagini and Richards in *Action*, is:

> *If they say to you:*
> *'You were out of where?'*
> *say to them:*
> *'We came out from the light,*
> *the place where the light has been—there—out of itself.*
> *It stood and showed itself out in their mold.'*
> *If they say to you:*
> *'You, that?',*
> *say to them:*
> *'We its children and we the chosen of the father who living.'*
> *If they question you:*
> *'What is the sign of your father in you?',*
> *say:*
> *'A movement it is and a repose.'*[13]
> *[. . .]*
> *I stood inbetween the world and I showed me out to them in meat.*
> *I did fall on all of them drunk, I did not fall on anyone among them who thirsts.*
> *It gives to my soul pain from the children of men,*
> *but blind men—those—in their heart!*
> *And they do not see, but they went into the world being empty,*
> *they seek even to go out of the world being empty,*
> *only that now they are drunk.*
> *When they shake off their wine, then they will change mind.*[14]
> *[. . .]*
> *—These little ones who are being suckled are like those who go in the kinghood.*
> *—Well then! If we little ones, we will go in the kinghood?*
> *—When you will have made the two one,*
> *and when you will have made the inner side as the outer side,*
> *and the outer side as the inner side,*

and the higher side as the lower side,
and so that you make the male and the female into one unique,
in order that the male will not do male nor the female do female;
when you will have made eyes in the place of an eye
and a hand in the place of hand
and a foot in the place of a foot,
a mold in the place of a mold,
then you will go in.[15]
[. . .]
Be passers-by.[16]
[. . .]
—Tell us, but our end will be how?
—Have you uncovered out, then, the beginning, that you look for the
end?
But in the place which is the beginning, there the end will be, there!
Blessed one is he who will stand at the beginning
and he will know the end and he will not get the taste of death.[17]

The syntax of the Workcenter translation, fragments of which are awkward at best in English, in fact often corresponds more closely to Polish syntax. For instance, 'Tell us, but our end will be how?' translated literally into Polish (Powiedz nam, ale nasz koniec będzie jaki?) or 'You are out of where?' (Jesteście skąd?), sound more natural in Polish and must have found a resonance with Grotowski's own underlying syntactical base.

The text of the Gospel of Thomas contains key themes which were already present in earlier phases of Grotowski's work, such as the notion of movement and repose, which surfaces in the Theatre of Sources, or the idea of being in the beginning, which also echoes Grotowski's earlier discussion of the art of the beginner. Beyond the key thematic threads that appear in the text, the Gospel of Thomas also provides interesting archetypal sources, which are reflected in Grotowski's relation to his close collaborators and the intimate symbiotic relationships prevalent in the work undertaken in the domain of Art as vehicle. These pairings, twinnings and couplings resemble the intimate spiritual twinship of Jesus and Thomas.

Thomas the Apostle is variously known as 'the twin' and 'Doubting Thomas'. The Gospel According to John establishes that others refer to Thomas as 'the twin' (11:16). The meaning of the Hebrew מואת (Toem)—from which 'Thomas' is derived—denotes twin, as does the Greek Didymus that appears as an epithet in the Gospel of Thomas. There is a multitude of doublings, as in the repetition of the word 'twin' in various languages, as well as the notion of Thomas as Jesus' twin, in the *Book of Thomas the Contender*, also part of the Nag Hammadi library:

> The savior said, 'Brother Thomas while you have time in the world, listen to me, and I will reveal to you the things you have pondered in your mind. Now, since it has been said that you are my twin and true companion, examine yourself, and learn who you are, in what way you exist, and how you will come to be. Since you will be called my brother, it is not fitting that you be ignorant of yourself. And I know that you have understood, because you had already understood that I am the knowledge of the truth. So while you accompany me, although you are uncomprehending, you have (in fact) already come to know, and you will be called "the one who knows himself". For he who has not known himself has known nothing, but he who has known himself has at the same time already achieved knowledge about the depth of the all. So then, you, my brother Thomas, have beheld what is obscure to men, that is, what they ignorantly stumble against' (Turner 1975).

Here the relation of twinship between Jesus and Thomas is closely tied to the process of self-examination and the discovery of the knowledge of truth through self-discovery. It is precisely in this process of self-discovery and active acquisition of self-knowledge that the kinship between the two men is established. Jesus calls Thomas to what is quintessentially a form of mimesis, and it is through the imitation of Jesus' behaviour that Thomas's twinship is solidified and fulfilled.

The mimetic relationship between Jesus and Thomas is not unlike the relation between doers in *Action*. The work that begins as a mimetic tuning-in to the process of another doer has the potential of transforming into a symbiotic connection between two or more doers in which the work on inner ascension is performed in tandem. Richards describes this type of connection as a 'horizontal' highway between two doers, which appears in relation to 'something third' (2008: 130). The process of attaining a 'horizontal' connection between doers may begin with the transmission of ritual song and movement and then develop into an internal mimesis aimed at the alignment of the doer's 'inner potentials to the unfolding process of the person who leads the song' (ibid.: 131). This process of horizontal alignment is directly tied to verticality. Once the horizontal connection is established, a shared vertical movement can take place between the two doers. Richards describes this process: 'I need to neutralize inside myself any element of our relationship that might block the face-to-face road, in order that his inner reservoir and mine can become like one, linked to the common intention of inner ascension. And here you have that highway starting to appear' (ibid.). The horizontal connection can be perceived as a form of 'twinning', becoming connected or developing an intimate connection in the vertical ascension.

One can look for analogies in the various twinnings that occur in the Grotowski work beginning with Grotowski's own intimate relationships with his close collaborators, such as Eugenio Barba, Zbigniew Cynkutis, Ryszard Cieślak[18] and Thomas Richards. While close collaborations with a particular individual are characteristic of different phases of Grotowski's work, it is important to emphasize that the nature of each work relationship was distinct. As Biagini points out, each collaboration was directed at a different and specific effort (2008: 152). One of the distinguishing characteristics of Grotowski's creative relationship with Richards is that, for the first time, Grotowski engaged in a 'conscious effort of transmission' (ibid.).

Of course, it is hard to overlook the coincidental reiteration of the name Thomas in the figure of Thomas Richards, with whom Grotowski shared the single longest collaboration, which lasted the latter 13 years of his life. References to the 'twinship' between Grotowski and Richards already circulate in recent scholarship on the work of Grotowski and the Workcenter. Antonio Attisani refers to Richards as Grotowski's 'elective twin' (2008: 99). Wolford Wylam remarks on the 'profoundly symbiotic dual identity' (2008: 132) of Grotowski and Richards by observing the montage of their pictures in the 1995 English publication of *At Work with Grotowski on Physical Actions*. On the cover image of the book, adjacent to the right side of Grotowski's face, appears the left side of Richard's face. The two split images create an uncanny juxtaposition of a grey-haired, bearded and ageing Grotowski with glasses with the youthful Richards. The dissimilarity of the dimensions of each image makes clear that a seamless montage was not the intended effect of this pairing. The size of

Richards' larger image creates the impression of a jutting forth or forward movement, which may easily be read as an act of situating Richards in the position of the one moving forward in time, in relation to the slightly distanced image of Grotowski, which recedes into the background. What unites the two images above all else is the at once focused and penetrating gaze of each, which points to a shared intensity and common vision.

What is more, this publication is framed both by a preface written by Grotowski and an important Grotowski essay, 'From the Theatre Company to Art as Vehicle' (1995a), which appears as an appendix. Wolford Wylam underscores the shared nature of the publication by suggesting that by writing the book's acknowledgments Grotowski participates in the authorial function (2008: 132). Grotowski's preface to the book is instrumental in authorizing Richards' words that follow. Wolford Wylam also recalls Grotowski reading to her from his interview conducted by Jean-Pierre Thibaudat, and lingering on one particular line which 'he translated as "[h]e is the man of research I was searching for", emphasizing Richards' agency as investigator, his pivotal role in both envisioning and embodying the praxis of Art as vehicle' (ibid.: 134).

The paradigm of Jesus and Thomas the Apostle as a spiritual twin[19] seems to pervade other work pairings between doers in the domain of Art as vehicle. The horizontal 'highway' described above by Richards refers also to his own close collaboration with Biagini, often characterized by both men as a brotherly relation. In *Heart of Practice*, Richards recalls his early work with Biagini, who appeared as 'B' in his work journal of the time. Biagini offers the following description of the work relation that began to emerge when he first began working directly with Richards and Grotowski: 'From that adventurous period, full of surprises, I remember the strange sensation that Grotowski was showing me the road toward finding my brother—a brother never met but always sought—the road toward perceiving and recognizing, toward opening my eyes' (2008: 153). While the metaphor of twinship or a nonfamilial use of the notion of brotherhood is certainly applicable here, in some circumstances the doer's biography might render this search more literal.

Biagini speaks of the process of an active and embodied search for one's brother or twin as a continuous questioning, associating this form of inquiry with the I-I discussed by Grotowski in his seminal essay 'Performer' (2010). Biagini suggests that the notion of I-I is, in part, a continuous questioning of 'who is the "I" that is doing?' and 'who is the "I" that is looking?' (2010). In a subsection of 'Performer' entitled 'The I-I', Grotowski states:

> It can be read in ancient texts: *We are two. The bird who picks and the bird who looks on. The one will die, the one will live.* Busy with picking, drunk with life inside time, we forgot to *make live* the part in us which looks on. So there is a danger to exist only inside time, and in no way outside time. To feel looked upon by this other part of yourself (the part which is outside time) gives another dimension. There is an I-I. The second I is quasi virtual; it is not—in you—the look of the others, nor any judgment; it's like an immobile look: a silent presence, like the sun which illuminates the things—and that's all. The process can be accomplished only in the context of this still presence. I-I: in experience, the couple doesn't appear as separate, but as full, unique (2001a: 378; emphasis in original).

In what follows, Grotowski goes on to elucidate the role of a teacher in the process of the development of an internal I-I relation. The 'looking presence' of a teacher has the potential of functioning as a 'mirror of the connection of I-I' (ibid.). Once this 'junction' or the 'channel I-I' has been traced or internalized, the teacher can disappear and Performer can continue on their own towards reaching the *body of essence*.[20]

Along similar lines as the relationship between Performer and teacher of Performer, the relation of twinship can be seen as an externalization of an inner I-I dynamic. The external relationship between twins can serve a mirroring function in which one can see the self reflected in the other. However, I would argue that the relation between twins, as formulated by Grotowski, disrupts conventional notions of relationality between the self and other. Instead of placing the emphasis on difference, the relation of twinship points to an identicalness, on both the linguistic level and in practice, bringing into focus the likeness connecting two human beings. It is not that within the relation of twinship difference is denied. Rather, the centre of gravity is firmly rooted in that which is shared—common qualities and, in the case of Grotowski's work, first and foremost a shared process of self-discovery and realization.

In the context of the work undertaken in the domain of Art as vehicle, the shared journey is formulated as a 'common intention of inner ascension' (Richards 2008: 131). A shared journey, of course, does not necessarily imply that two people are at the same point of development. Moreover, the position and function of each doer may vary in relation to the other. The role of each doer, whether more active or passive, is fluid and fluctuates: '[T]he active/passive division is never so clear-cut. There are moments when active and passive are shifting in terms of the inner charge of ascension, but that's more complicated' (ibid.).

There is yet another aspect of the brotherly or teacher-student relation that may facilitate the process of discovery through doing. Richards describes a game he used to play as a nine-year-old, when he sought contact with his older brother:

> My brother would be upstairs in his room. I was looking for contact with him. I would go upstairs very quietly into his room and start making a sound: tick tock tick tock tick [. . .]. And I'd start to move in a very odd way, almost dancing around his room. He would say to me, 'Tick Tock, please clean my room.' And I would say 'Yes, yes, tick tock, tick tock. . . .' And I would start to clean his room—make his bed, clean the floor, do everything—and he would give me a raisin. I'd open my mouth and he'd put the raisin inside. And I would go on, 'tick tock tick tock,' and continue dancing around the room (ibid.: 48).

Richards describes the horror with which his parents viewed this oppressive pastime, and acknowledges this aspect of the game. However, as he goes on to explain, his perception of this experience as a nine-year-old was entirely different. For Richards, the experience of doing something for his brother was one of extraordinary liberation:

> I was doing *for him*, he was my brother, and everything made sense. I don't know why. It was not filtered through my mind, that this was right or this was wrong. It was just working. And I was dancing—so free! And doing things perfectly, much more perfectly than when I was doing for myself when I cleaned my own room. Some nourishment came from him. He gave me some food. But it was not just the raisin, it was the connection, what was passing from him to me in that moment. So I can see that in that moment in my life, it was like I was looking for my teacher (ibid.: 49; emphasis in original).

The childhood game described by Richards reveals an important dimension of doing for or in relation to an other, along with the potentialities that this relational action opens up, which is also pertinent to the twinship relations in the domain of Art as vehicle. The intentionality of doing for an other liberates hidden potentialities of the doer. In letting go of doing for the self, the ego is loosened and a way of doing emerges which is perceived as 'more perfect', one which is experienced as 'extraordinary freedom and joy' (ibid.). For it is in the intentionality of doing for something other than the self that an opening emerges: 'And from that "for something else", some possibility is liberated, some channel opens' (ibid.). The playful dance or doing for someone or something other than oneself is initiated by a desire for contact with an other and is nourished by that very contact.

An interesting expression of twinship also emerges in the work that was developed in the Workcenter after Grotowski's death, namely in *The Twin: An Action in Creation*.[21] In this opus, there exists a close interrelation between Richards and another doer, Souphiène Amiar. A native of Algeria, Amiar bears a remarkable physical resemblance to Richards. This twinning, albeit coincidental, approaches an almost literal twinship or doubling, in which the process of transmission from one doer to another (Richards to Amiar) is gradually transformed into a joining of two doers in a shared movement along a vertical axis.

While a narrative reading of opuses created in the domain of Art as vehicle is not the centre of gravity of the works, there is a deep interrelation between the textual, physical and vocal aspects of these pieces and the structuring of internal intentions and associations along with the process of inner ascension. The primary text of *The Twin: An Action in Creation* is a manuscript also belonging to the Gnostic Acts of Thomas. 'The Hymn of the Pearl', alternatively known as 'The Hymn of the Robe of Glory', is a Gnostic Poem that recounts the myth of the exile and redemption of the soul. Originally composed in old Syriac, 'The Hymn of the Pearl' is attributed by scholars variously to the Syrian Gnostic Bardaisan (*c*.154–222 CE) or a Bardesanist poet (Mead 1908).[22]

The poem tells the story of a Prince who must journey from the East to Egypt to recover from the sea a pearl guarded by a 'loud-breathing Serpent'. The Prince is sent on this quest by his parents, while his brother ('the Second') remains home in the kingdom. Once the compact is made between the Prince and his parents it is inscribed in his heart so that he does not forget. The Prince ventures out with provisions from his home accompanied by two couriers;

however, when he arrives in the land of Egypt the escorts depart and he is left to journey alone. Immediately upon entry into Egypt, the Prince—his mind still focused and resolute—goes straight to the Serpent. He plans to wait until it falls asleep so he can take the pearl. While waiting, he meets a kinsman whom he makes his 'chosen companion' and a 'comrade, for sharing my wares with' (ibid.: VI). Here, I read 'wares' in the archaic sense, denoting the keeping of vigil. But then the Prince comes into contact with the local Egyptians and begins to forget about his quest, succumbing to a deep sleep 'from the weight of their victuals' (ibid.: VII). Fortuitously, his parents perceive the Prince's sleep and send a letter—on behalf of themselves and the Second Brother—urging the Prince to remember his true identity and his quest for the pearl. At this point in the poem there is a description full of beautiful imagery of the letter transforming into an Eagle and flying to the Prince:

XI.

It flew in the form of the Eagle,
Of all the winged tribes the king-bird;

It flew and alighted beside me,
And turned into speech altogether.

At its voice and the sound of its winging,
I waked and arose from my deep sleep.

Unto me I took it and kissed it;
I loosed its seal and I read it.

E'en as it stood in my heart writ,
The words of my Letter were written.

XII.

I remembered that I was a King's son,
And my rank did long for its nature.

I bethought me again of the Pearl,
For which I was sent down to Egypt.

And I began [then] to charm him,
The terrible loud-breathing Serpent.

I lulled him to sleep and to slumber,
Chanting o'er him the Name of my Father,

The Name of our Second, [my Brother],
And [Name] of my Mother, the East-Queen.

(Mead 1908)

This depiction is reminiscent of Grotowski's notion that the rediscovery of essence is experienced as a memory. It can be characterized as a reawakening from a deep slumber to the experience of essence; a remembering of that which is already there, written in the heart. The written epistle is sent in the form of an eagle which transfigures the written word into speech. The sound of the words, in turn, awakens the Prince. They stir that which is already written within him, the words of the compact inscribed in his heart. The trajectory is a perpetual movement and transfiguration of the written into the spoken word, of awakening and sleep, and of forgetting and remembering.

While the Prince manages to awaken from slumber with the aid of the epistle borne by the Eagle, sleep is also the weapon with which he lulls the Serpent. Whereas the sound of the enunciated words of the letter sent from his kingdom serve to waken him, it is the chanting of the names of his parents and brother that induces the Serpent to sleep. The utterance of words acts both to awaken and to lull to sleep.

Once the Serpent is asleep, the Prince snatches the pearl and returns to his home guided by the light of the letter: 'As with its voice it had roused me, So now with its light it did lead me' (ibid.: XIII). Upon his return home, the Prince dons his Glorious Robe, which he had taken off prior to his journey. The robe has the image of the 'King of Kings' depicted on it and becomes a mirror for the Prince, who recognizes himself reflected in the bejewelled robe:

At once, as soon as I saw it,
The Glory looked like my own self.
XVI.

I saw it in all of me,
And saw me all in [all of] it,—

That we were twain in distinction,
And yet again one in one likeness.

> I saw, too, the Treasurers also,
> Who unto me had down-brought it,
>
> Were twain [and yet] of one likeness;
> For one Sign of the King was upon them—
>
> Who through them restored me the Glory,
> The Pledge of my Kingship [?]
>
> (ibid.: XI–XVI)

At this juncture, the Robe assumes the function of the Twin by serving as a reflection of the Prince's likeness. Moreover, the robe has the 'motions of Gnosis abounding' all over it (ibid.: XVIII). The Prince sees the robe preparing as if to speak and hears the music that it whispers as it descends towards him:

> 'Behold him the active in deeds!
> For whom I was reared with my Father;
>
> 'I too have felt in myself
> How that with his works waxed my stature.'
>
> (ibid.: XVIII)

The narrative, and indeed the Robe itself, seems to insinuate a brotherly relation between the Robe and the Prince. One reading of the story might suggest that the first brother, the Prince, the 'active in deeds', is the external manifestation or embodiment of the 'twain in distinction, but one in likeness'. The Second Brother who stays behind in the Kingdom is the eye who perceives the Prince and awakens him from sleep and to the memory of his true identity and quest. Wolford Wylam refers to the Second Brother as the Prince's 'vigilant twin, the Brother who remembers everything' (2008: 141).

The figure of the brother, or the Twin, is the synthesis and symbolic embodiment of three notions explored thus far in this book: memory and remembering, vigilance and the externalization of the I-I dynamic to which Grotowski gestures in 'Performer'. The Second Brother, figured as an externalization of the I-I relationship, acts as the external eye, as the one who remains vigilant when the brother 'active in deeds' falls into a sleep that also marks a forgetting of that which is already inscribed in the heart. The vigilant brother is able to rouse the Prince and remind him of the quest that he has set upon. So while the brother 'active in deeds' is not relieved of the responsibility to remember and remain vigilant, the Second Brother functions as a mechanism that ensures the return to memory and vigilance if the Prince temporarily falters.

Alongside the interpersonal relations that exist within the research in the domain of Art as vehicle, there are many structural elements of the work that serve the same function as the vigilant twin. There are, of course, the precise vocal, physical and internal scores that serve as the structural basis for vertical ascension. In Chapter 1, I have already remarked upon the importance of the deep—if not overt—connection between the various dimensions of the internal and external score and the meaning of the spoken text.

In the context of *An Action in Creation*, the textual component of the 'Hymn of the Pearl' becomes particularly significant: 'Unlike previous Actions, in which the process of inner ascension is approached primarily through song, spoken text predominates in *An Action in Creation*, with the quest story repeated multiple times in fragments, a refrain that functions for the doers as a tool to aid in remembering their purpose' (Wolford Wylam 2008: 141). Thus the textual elements of this performance function as a continuous multidimensional reminder. In the work of Art as vehicle, the text or narrative may also function as a tool in movement on the vertical itinerary. Richards argues that it is not the *form* of a narrative that is pivotal in this context, but its content: 'Working with certain meanings, we operate with another vehicle that can enter and become part of an access to verticality' (2008: 162). The signification of a given text, and what one is able to extract from it, is explored in the performative work through a repeated encounter with the text within the context of structured and tightly scored embodied actions (ibid.: 162).

The relation to the text itself and its use within the performative structure of *An Action in Creation* is more interrogatory than declarative. Richards describes a possible point of entry into the making the 'Hymn of the Pearl' meaningful to the present moment:

What might this story be about? There is a journey from the East, the 'land of rising,' down to a foreign country and the return. Might it refer to an inner journey? If yes, the question is, is it possible to enact this again? And how? Maybe the story is about each one of us. The sleep of stupor is here now. The devouring serpent is here now. And what about the pearl, the Brother with his capacity of remembering, and the doorway to the house of the Father? Are they also here? Maybe this foreign land is here now. It's our daily life. And the letter sent form the East to the Prince to wake him up, maybe it is also here. The story is circular. It begins at the door of the East and ends there. How do we incorporate it into our lives, how do we dialogue with it, if possible? On this level, the narrative form is important simply because the text's content is articulated in the form of a story (ibid.: 162–3).

Therefore, it is the dialogical engagement with the meanings contained in a given text that serve as instruments with the potential of moving one along a vertical axis. In the domain of Art as vehicle, the movement along a vertical itinerary is intimately tied to a continuous vigilance and active remembering. There emerge at least three discernible and distinct ways in which the process of active remembering and vigilance is facilitated. The first is the structural aspect of the work, such as internal and external scoring of performative structures. The second consists of the various elements deployed in the work, which range from traditional songs and movements of the Afro-Caribbean line to texts from Gnostic Apocryphal literature. The third component of the work, which brings the doer back to her intended purpose of inner ascension, is the I-I relation. This relationship is at first externalized in the teacher-apprentice dynamic, in which the teacher functions as the outside eye, reminding and reawakening the student when she slumbers. This external relationship is also embodied in other pairings of the doers themselves, between the more experienced work leaders and the novices. Yet it is also the dynamic that manifests itself in the reciprocal work relation between doers.

In regards to the relation between brothers or twins as the external I-I dynamic, it is interesting to note that Grotowski no longer refers to Martin Buber's concept of I and Thou (*Ich und Du*) (1958). This conceptual shift from I-Thou to I-I marks not only a narrowing of distance between the self and the other but also underscores the likeness between the self and the external world, as well as the reflective or mirroring function of the I-I relation. Buber differentiates between two ways in which the human being engages with the world. The first is through the I-it relation, a subject-to-object relation, in which human beings perceive themselves as separate and detached entities surrounded by objects. The I-it relation allows the subject to perceive only the specific and isolatable qualities of objects. In contrast, Buber's notion of the I-Thou relation is a subject-subject relation which allows one to perceive the totality of another. Although dialogical and reciprocal in nature, Buber's I-Thou relation is envisioned as one which allows for an experience of an essential unity between two or more subjects. This relation is direct, unmediated and not encumbered by the separation of an intervening set of ideas. The notion of I-I, as the terminological shift itself suggests, places an even greater emphasis on the twinship or likeness between two relational subjects.

Following Buber's distinction between two modes of engagement with the world as characterized by either a subject-object relation and a subject-subject relation, it might be tempting to categorize the various tools deployed in the domain of Art as vehicle as falling into two groups. The doers' engagement with traditional songs, ritual movements or texts might fall under the rubric of subject-object relations, and interpersonal encounters configured as an externalized I-I dynamic would be exemplary of the subject-subject relationship. However, the actual praxis conducted in the domain of Art as vehicle problematizes such dichotomous distinctions, for cultural artifacts such as traditional Afro-Haitian songs are not treated as objects but as subjects. The song is often referred to as a person, a grandmother or another ancient relative. Such blurring of the object-subject differentiation disrupts the dichotomy of human relationality put forward by Buber, among others.

Furthermore, this unsettling of an I-it relation may, in fact, shed light on Grotowski's shift from the conceptual framework of Buber's I-Thou to the I-I. Grotowski's adoption of the I-I in place of the I-Thou implies a blurring of boundaries between the I and the Other. Whether internal or external, the I-I designates a relationship of likeness or twinship. The I-I is a repetition of an identical I, and while the hyphen does necessarily impose a separation, there is an underlying unity between the two. The hyphen which splits the *Is*, whether perceived as the connective tissue or severing cut between the two, certainly implies differentiation, a quality without which relationality would not be possible. However, the two entities held on opposite sides of the equation now bear a more remarkable resemblance to one another than the I-it and the I-Thou relation.

The move to obscure boundaries between the Self and Other, between subject and object—a concept pervasive in some Eastern philosophies[23]—may be unsettling to those acculturated in the West or trained in Western philosophies and sciences, and particularly psychology and psychoanalysis. While the concept may unhinge contemporary Western worldviews, this notion is clearly already present in the early Christian Gnostic tradition. For instance, the mysterious transfiguration of the Second Brother into the glorious robe ('That we were twain in distinction, And yet again one in one likeness' [Mead 1908: XVI]) with which the Prince proceeds to enrobe himself ('And my Mantle of sparkling colours I wrapped entirely all o'er me' [ibid.: XIX]) symbolically dissolves the subject-object divide. The robe bears the image of the King of Kings, in which the Prince recognizes himself. The Prince recounts how his love urged forward to run to meet the robe and receive it: 'I clothed me therewith, and ascended to the Gate of Greeting and Homage' (ibid.: XX). In this scenario, the Second Brother (subject) is transfigured into the Glorious Robe (object), which in turn merges again with the Prince (subject).

The relation of the Prince in the 'Hymn of the Pearl' can thus be characterized as a relationality of the externalized I-I (the subject-subject relationship between the Prince and the Second Brother, his vigilant Twin), which, with the Second Brother's transfiguration into the Robe, is transformed into a subject-object relation. Once the Prince receives the robe, the two entities seem to merge into one, as he recognizes himself in the image on the Robe and wraps himself with it. Thus, the living being represented by the Second Brother, the subject, is continuous with an object. The Prince's encounter with the world is that of an I-I relationality throughout, with the external I/eye shifting shapes and subject/object positions. All of the subjects and objects he encounters— his Second Brother, the epistle-turned-Eagle and, finally, his Robe—serve a similar function: to mirror his image so that he may recognize his true identity. These encounters stir him from slumber and reawaken him to that which is already written in his heart, and return him to his quest. Grotowski's use of the I-I blurs the boundaries of the Self and Other, subject and object, while simultaneously retaining the necessary split between the two I's which correspond with two eyes: one internal and one external.

There is yet another link binding the text of the 'Hymn of the Pearl' to Grotowski's notion of Performer. The words uttered by the robe in reference to the Prince, 'Behold him the active in deeds', are reminiscent of Grotowski's understanding of Performer as 'a man of action. [. . .] He is a doer, a priest a warrior: outside aesthetic genres' (2001a: 376). In the next chapter I will continue my consideration of Grotowski's notions and practices associated with relationality, this time in the context of intercultural transmission.

Notes

1 In the introduction to his book *Wielki mały wóz* (Big Small Vehicle) Leszek Kolankiewicz conducts an etymological analysis of the term 'vehicle' (2001). Beyond the common denotations of 'carrier' and 'transmitter', vehicle from the Latin *vehiculum* is a medium of a suitable kind in which strong or unpalatable drugs or medicines are administered. Kolankiewicz also draws attention to the resonance with the Buddhist notions of Mahayana and Hinayana (big and small vehicle) from the Sanskrit *yana* denoting vehicle or path. Hinayana is usually used to designate the path leading to the achievement of Nirvana (personal liberation) as opposed to Mahayana, which leads to the liberation of Samyaksabuddha (spiritual liberation of all sentient beings from the suffering of samsara).

2 In the context of the Objective Drama programme, the term 'drama', in addition to referring to the enactment of scripted texts, is conceived more broadly and designates 'the performative impulse in all its forms' (Wolford 1991: 166).

3 For a more detailed treatment of the Polish term *człowiek poznania* see my discussion in Chapter 1.

4 This talk was given during a panel entitled 'Grotowski and Kantor' presented as part of Tracing Grotowski's Path: The Year of Grotowski in New York. Osiński's presentation was comprised of several longer texts abbreviated and edited by Professor Daniel Gerould. I translated the lecture from Polish into English.

5 Grotowski returns to this story on numerous occasions. Beside the film of *Nienadówka*, other instances include a 1975 interview conducted by Andrzej Bonarski first printed in *Kultura* (1979), as well as an article entitled 'Theatre of Sources', which appears in *The Grotowski Sourcebook* (2001: 252–70).

6 The first Polish publication of this work, *Żywot Jezusa*, translated by A. Niemojewski, was available in 1904.

7 Wanda Dynowska's Polish translation of this work appeared just before the Second World War in 1939 with the Polish title *Ścieżkami jogów*.

8 All translations from this source are mine.

9 While in Theatre School in Kraków from 1 October 1951 to 30 June 1955, Grotowski consulted with Helena Willman-Grabowska who specialized in Indian and Iranian

culture as well as Franciszek Tokarz, an expert in Indian philosophy (Osiński 1986: 14).

10 In the period between 1957 and 1959, while working actively as a theatre director in Kraków, Grotowski gave a series of public lectures on 'Oriental philosophy' at Theatre 38 (Osiński 1986: 21). The scope of these lectures spanned Chinese, Japanese and Indian philosophies as well as their European 'analogies', and included topics such as Zen Buddhism, Confucianism, Taoism and Advaita Vedanta.

11 Yoga practice constituted one of the points of departure for the physical exercises developed by Grotowski and the Laboratory Theatre actors during the Theatre of Productions phase. Altered versions of hatha yoga *asanas* (poses) were the basis for many of the physical exercises described in *Towards a Poor Theatre*. A dynamic or flowing sequence of these poses coupled with work on personal associations, known as plastiques or corporals, is demonstrated by Ryszard Cieślak in the film documenting his work with actors of Odin Teatret (Wethal 1971).

12 Renan's work presents Jesus as an extraordinarily noble human being possessing only the best qualities and intentions, but only a human being nevertheless. The work's systematic demystification of the divine nature of Jesus is undoubtedly the reason for its illicit status in the eyes of the Roman Catholic Church.

13 The Workcenter's translation appears in Attisani (2006). The following is an interlinear Coptic/English translation by Michael W. Grondin (2002):

> Said this: 'If they should speak to you (pl) this: "Have you come into being out (of) where?" Speak to them this "We have come out of the light, the place which the light came into being there, outward by his hand himself; he stood to his feet and he appeared forth in their image". If they should speak to you (pl) this "You (pl) are (him)?", speak this "We (are) his sons, and we (are) the chosen of the father who lives". If they should ask yourselves this: "What is the sign of your (pl) father which is in yourselves?", speak to them this "A movement it is, and a repose."'

14 Grondin's translation:

> Said this: 'Did I stand to my feet in the midst of the world, and did I appear outwardly to them in flesh. Did I fall upon them, all of them, () drunk; did not I fall on anyone among them () thirsting; and did my soul give pain over the sons of men, for () blind men (they) are in their mind, and they look outward not, for they have come to the world () empty; they seek also that they come out of the world () empty; but now

they are drunk; when they should shake off their wine, then they will repent' (2002).

15 Grondin's translation:

Did look at some little ones () taking milk. Said he to his disciples this: 'These little ones who take milk, they compare to those who go in to the kingdom'. Said they to him this: 'Then, () being little ones, we will go into the kingdom?' Said to them this: 'When you (pl) should make the two one, and if you (pl) should make the side inner like the side outer, and the side outer like the side inner, and the side upper like the side lower, and so you (pl) will be making the male and the woman that one alone, so that not the male become male, (nor) the woman become woman; when you (pl) should make some eyes to the place of an eye, and a hand to the place of a hand, and a foot to the place of a foot; an image to the place of an image, then you (pl) will go into the kingdom' (2002).

16 Grondin's translation: 'Said this: "Come into being as you (pl) pass away"' (2002).

17 Grondin's translation:

Said the disciples to (JS) this: 'Speak to us this our end, she will come to be in which way?'. Said (this) 'Have you (pl) revealed (), forth the beginning, so that you (pl) will be seeking after the end? For in the place which the beginning (is) there, the end will come to be there; a blessed one, he who will stand to his feet in the beginning, and he will know the end, and he will take taste not of death' (2002)

18 Ferdinando Taviani characterizes Grotowski's collaborative work with Cieślak on *The Constant Prince* as one producing the compound entity of Grotowski-Cieślak (Taviani 2009; Wolford Wylam 2008).

19 The Polish term *bliźnię* (twin) does not necessarily denote the quantity of two. It is proper usage to say *trzecie, czwarte bliźnię* (third, fourth 'twin'). Etymologically speaking *bliźnięta* (twins) are *bliźne* or *bliskie* (close; closely related). The Old Polish *bliźny* has been replaced by *bliźni* or *krewny* (blood relative). In biblical usage and Christian ethic every human being is *bliźny* in relation to the other.

20 For a fuller discussion of Grotowski's notion the *body of essence* see Chapter 1.

21 In 2005 'The Twin' was eliminated from the title, from which point the opus was known simply as *An Action in Creation* (Wolford Wylam 2008: 140).

22 Syrian-Egyptian Gnostic Schools were ancient Gnostic sects from the Middle East, which drew heavily on Platonic and Judaic traditions. Bardaisan was a Syriac

gnostic, founder of the Bardaisanites, and an outstanding scientist, scholar, astrologist, philosopher and poet. He was renowned for his knowledge of India.

23 Hinduism concedes phenomenological diversity but posits absolute unity on the metaphysical level (Brahman) and, as Ashok Vohra argues, contains no notion of the other (2003: 93). *Itai Doshin*, the Buddhist notion of unity, also acknowledges the diversity and uniqueness of each sentient being, while emphasizing their interconnectedness through the concept of 'different body, same spirit'. The Taoist principle of the unity of opposites is yet another example of the interconnectedness of phenomena and metaphysical unity in Eastern philosophies and religions.

'Let Me Take You to the Land of Your Ancestors'

Grotowski and Transmission

> Singing is a need. In my case, it corresponds to a need for fusion, a connection, a melting within something that is universal and timeless. Then there appears a chance that something which is very deep will resonate. I spend whole hours singing for just one single second of feeling connected. A connection is also a rootedness. When one is rooted there is a greater potential to be connected with the life sources (Robart 2001: 250).[1]

On 2 September 1802, at two in the afternoon, ships carrying the 3rd Polish Demibrigade anchored in Cap Français, Haiti.[2] They constituted the first wave of Polish Legionnaires[3] sent by Napoleon Bonaparte at the urgent request of his brother-in-law General Charles Leclerc, in command of the colonial military campaign in St Domingue.[4] The Polish Legions, accompanied by German and Swiss contingents, were sent to aid the French forces in the suppression of the slave uprising.[5] Factions of the Polish Legionnaires became sympathetic to the cause of the slave uprising and defected, joining the freedom fighters.

Haitian historian Thomas Madiou, referring to the St Marc massacre, observes that 'the Polish troops had fought with little enthusiasm against the indigenous forces since attempts had been made to re-establish slavery. They proudly declared that only military duty could induce them to burn their gunpowder against freedom' (in Pachoński and Wilson 1986: 105).[6] While the actual desertion rate among the Polish Legionnaires was lower than popular legend suggests, to this day it is still widely believed in Haiti that significant numbers of Poles supported Jean-Jacques Dessalines, one of the rebellion leaders, and that entire units changed sides along with their officers (ibid.: 311). According to Tadeusz Łepkowski, approximately 120–50 legionnaires joined the insurgents voluntarily (ibid.). At the time of the French retreat in 1803, 4,000 of the 5,280 Poles sent to St Domingue were dead due to drowning, yellow fever or combat. While 700 returned to France and 200 emigrated to Cuba and the United States, approximately 400 stayed on the island by defecting to the former slave revolutionaries, intermarrying with the local women or being taken prisoner (Rypson 2008: 14–15).

Notwithstanding the discrepancies between divergent historical accounts and popular beliefs about the role of Polish Legionnaires in the Haitian revolution, the Poles acquired special status as evidenced by Articles 12 and 13 of the Haitian Constitution of 1805, which states that, along with Germans, they are the only whites with the right to own property in Haiti. In response to a question about their future status, Dessalines is reported to have said: 'The Poles are to be accepted as children of the island, naturalize all who wish to remain with us' (Pachoński and Wilson 1986: 312).

Some historians claim that after independence, Polish deserters were, in fact, given land property in Cazale (ibid.: 311). While the Poloné-Ayisyen (Polish Haitians) live dispersed throughout Haiti to this day, there are concentrations in several villages, including St Jean du Sud, Fond des Blancs, La Baleine and Port Salut in the Southern peninsula (Rypson 2008: 22). Situated inland north-east of the main Port-au-Prince–St Marc road, Cazale is the largest Poloné village and most significant for this narrative. Of present-day residents of Cazale, Pachoński and Wilson write, 'Cazale's people are friendly enough, though shy. Many are unmistakably Polish in feature: some are blond and blue-eyed; some have high cheekbones and tapering chins' (1986: 313).

Listed among the Polish Legionnaires sent to quell the slave uprising is a certain F. Grotowski. Captain Feliks Grotowski figures little in the historical accounts of the Polish Legionnaire presence in Haiti. However, it is documented, for instance, that at the age of 25, with the 4th company under his command, he was assigned to convoy supplies to a French detachment (250 men) that Scylla and his Congos had surrounded at Marmelade (west of Dondon)(ibid.: 88).[7] After successfully reaching his objective, Captain Grotowski negotiated an agreement with the black chieftain Scylla that allowed him and his company to retreat safely in exchange for pledging to leave Scylla's storehouses intact (ibid.). Grotowski was ordered to take his company to Acul du Nord where on 7 October 1802 he joined the rest of General A. Clervaux's brigade, to which the Poles were assigned. It is here that the trail of the historical account of Captain Grotowski breaks off.

And it is here that the story of mythologized Grotowski(s) begins. In a talk entitled 'Grotowski's Second Homeland: Haiti'[8] given during the inauguration of the Year of Grotowski in Wrocław, Leszek Kolankiewicz recalls that Jerzy Grotowski liked to imagine that he was related to Captain Feliks Grotowski (2009). Zbigniew Osiński corroborates that it was one of Grotowski's fore-fathers, Feliks Grotowski, who took part in the battles of St Domingue (in Rypson 2008: 142). What is more, according to Kolankiewicz, Jerzy Grotowski liked to imagine that Capitan Feliks Grotowski was among those who joined the slave uprising in St Domingue. It is clear that from a historical perspective this is unlikely, since, with a few exceptions, high ranking officers did not join the insurgency. Pachoński and Wilson argue that Polish officers would have considered defection highly dishonourable and a contravention of their oath of loyalty to France (1986: 312). Osiński recalls a conversation with Jerzy Grotowski that he had in Italy during which Grotowski spoke with the highest regard about the Polish Legionnaires who joined the slave uprising stating 'that it was one of the most beautiful pieces of Polish history, and unfortunately not known at all' (in Rypson 2008: 142).

Whether Feliks Grotowski was Jerzy's blood relation or whether the Cap-tain actually joined the slave revolutionaries' fight for freedom is less important in the context of this study than the narrative that Jerzy Grotowski constructed for himself—and shared with others, as Kolankiewicz asserts.[9] What is signifi-cant, moreover, are the ways in which this contructed narrative influenced Grotowski's perception of his own identity and sense of belonging. I will in no way try to purport that it is possible to excavate Grotowski's perception of self, which self-evidently was not static througout his lifelong intense personal and professional development. One could attempt to begin to sketch an admit-tedly limited portrait of Grotowski, but this would require a kaleidoscopic view comprised of testimonies of many of his friends, colleagues and collaborators. Kolankiewicz's testimony is obviously a subjective recollection of the talks he had with Grotowski when the paratheatrical period—in which Kolankiewicz participated—and Theatre of Sources overlapped. What seems clear, however, is that the deep and complex connections between Grotowski and Haiti, to which Kolankiewicz's testimony gestures, are ones which Grotowski himself charted.

Grotowski's purported predilection for imagining that he was a relative of Captain Grotowski, as well as the possible line of action the Captain might have taken within the historical context of the Polish Legions' presence in St

Domingue, is indicative of Grotowski's own desires. The possible connection that Grotowski might have forged with Captain Grotowski in his mind carries more weight than any authentication of a 'real' blood relation. Beyond doubt is that, alongside what might have been a more fanciful creation of links to Haiti, Grotowski had a strong fascination for the country and its culture, which began at least as early as 1966.[10] Over the years, Grotowski forged real ties with Haiti not only through his travels there (the first visit in December 1977) but also through a sustained collaboration with Haitians, most notably with Jean-Claude 'Tiga' Garoute (1935–2006) and Maud Robart (b. 1946), cofounders and leaders of the Haitian community of Saint-Soleil, an artist collective established in 1974. What is more, Grotowski's interest in what he perceived as ancient African songs and ritual movements concentrated on its diasporic articulation and particularly the Afro-Haitian line of transmission. The ritual songs and movements associated with Haitian Vodou became the primary cultural artifacts or practical tools deployed by Grotowski in the last two decades of his research into ritual song. To this day, the Haitian line constitutes the fundamental performative vocabulary at the Workcenter of Jerzy Grotowski and Thomas Richards.

The motivating factors of Grotowski's visit to Haiti cannot be limited to a single purpose. Undoubtedly, he was conducting practical research that later became known as the Theatre of Sources (1976–82). During that phase, Grotowski sought embodied practices present in various traditions and explored their effect on people who were not of that specific culture. It was Grotowski's belief—further elaborated in the Objective Drama phase—that certain 'ancient' ritual actions had an effect on people that was 'objective', that is, separate from any cultural context. The actions, sounds, songs, and gestures in and of themselves are efficacious. Of course, the assertion of transcultural efficacy of actions has been challenged widely. It is not my intention to deal with those challenges here, but to trace Grotowski's own work in the terms that he himself prescribed. In addition to his travels to Haiti, Grotowski had made other expeditions to India, Nigeria, Mexico and within rural Poland.

Putting the motivational forces that brought Grotowski to Haiti aside for the moment, let us examine other sources, which tell a different story. Pachoński and Wilson, in passing, make the following comment: 'In Cazale the authors met a man who had spent eight months in Poland in 1980 visiting a

FIGURE 17: Amon Frémon. Photograph by Marek Musiał.

Polish gentleman who had come to Cazale "looking for his ancestors'" (1986: 316). Riccardo Orizio, who visited Cazale as part of the fieldwork conducted for his book *Lost White Tribes*, also makes mention of this man, but his narrative is more elaborate. The man is a houngan by the name of Amon Frémon,[11] a Vodou priest from Cazale. Orizio quotes Frémon's account of his encounter with the Polish visitor:

> My grandfather was Polish; his name was Faon Frémon Beké. My father was Polish. I am Polish. And I went to Poland because I was invited to go by Jerzy Detopski. Who was he? *Un blanc* who had come to Casales [Cazale] to look for any surviving relatives and take them back to Poland to meet his family. Jerzy was an important man, *un grand blanc*. Well, he chose me. I went all over Poland, but they took me to France, to Paris, too. I don't know if Jerzy is still alive today, and I reckon there's no way I could find out. Take you and me for example. Here we are chatting together today, and maybe you die tomorrow.

Who can tell. As we say, birds come and go, eating the crumbs we scatter. What was Poland like? There was snow and lots of forests. No, I didn't stay there, because the curfew came along and the white man sent me back home. I'm still fond of Jerzy, because he did a lot of nice things for me and always saw that everything was just so. I still love him even though I don't know where he is now. [. . .] When I was in Poland I didn't have to spend any money at all. The *blanc* paid for everything (in Orizio 2000: 142–3).[12]

Why was Frémon chosen by Jerzy to return to Poland?

'Jerzy chose me because he liked the way I lived. I'm a magic-man, I have special powers, everyone here loves me. And the *grand blanc* liked the idea of a Pole who knew about magic.'

[. . .] 'Look,' he said, 'Jerzy knew that I was the one man who could bring peace to Poland. The country was up in arms and needed someone with magic powers. Jerzy took me all over the place, to one city after another, and organized great festivals of magic. Every city we went to, we would take at least 25 white men with us into the forest and perform rites together.' He broke off suddenly, as if he had suddenly recollected an incident that would not bear the telling, and concluded by saying, 'Ah no, mine is not an easy profession.' (ibid.: 143)

In Orizio's account, Jerzy's last name is notated as Detopski.

Sebastian Rypson cites another, slightly altered account of this story that appears in *La Présence Polonaise en Haiti* (1983). The same man, Amon Frémon, is interviewed, but this time the details of the narrative diverge in several respects. For one, the mysterious Pole is now identified by the name Blokowski, which coincidentally also happens to be the surname of Amon Frémon's grandmother (Rypson 2008: 133). However, in all accounts, the Polish gentleman's given name, Jerzy, remains. The story is cited yet again, this time in Ian Thomson's *Bonjour Blanc* (1992). In the version recounted by Thomson, the man interviewed is also Frémon and the name of the Pole in question again appears as Blokowski.

Today, a small heritage of Poland survives in Cazales through dance and music. An elderly inhabitant of Belno, Amon Fremon, beat on a drum for us the rhythm of a minuet which derives from the polka. It is known up here as the 'Kokoda', a sort of Polish-Haitian half-step.

Monsieur Fremon is a Vodou priest. [. . .] Inside, the sanctum was hung with charms against the *mal jok*, evil eye: a goat's skull, objects shaped like twisted red peppers (the same amulets are to be found in Naples), countless plastic dolls like speechless mannequins with lidless eyes. 'I spent eight months in Warsaw,' the priest informed us. 'A Pole came here in search of his relatives. He shared my grandfather's surname—Blokowski. So he said, "Let me take you to the land of your ancestors." That was in 1980 and I'd never been on an aeroplane before.' 'What did you make of Warsaw?' 'Not bad. Wonderful vodka.' (Thomson 1992: 54–5).

The ensuing layer in the palimpsest of narratives documenting the meeting between Frémon and Jerzy is from the point of view of the Haitian houngan. It is this account that finally reveals Jerzy ——ski's true identity. Sebastian Rypson's study *Being Poloné in Haiti* (2008) is based on fieldwork conducted in Cazale in 2003. When Rypson questioned people in Cazale about ——ski's visit, someone responded: 'Wi, wi, Blokosky, li te vini isit-la pou prann gangan-nan Laba LaPoloy' ['Yes, yes, Blokosky, he came here to take the Vodou priest to Poland'] (2008: 136).

But it was, in fact, an anecdote told by Rypson's father that finally pointed to the true identity of the mysterious visitor to Cazale. In the early 1980s Piotr Rypson was sitting in a street cafe in Warsaw drinking an espresso and reading a newspaper when he saw a commotion forming around a group of Haitians walking in their 'tropical colours through the main street. I ask a neighbour what's going on and someone else answers, ah, it's probably Grotowski at it again' (ibid.: 138). Sebastian Rypson verified the hypothesis that Blokowski-Detopski was in fact Grotowski by 'holding up various downloaded portraits of Grotowski, which were met with much enthusiasm. In Haiti, the phonetic "r" is either a French "r", an English "w", or an "l"–sound' (ibid.: 139).

Grotowski did, in fact, visit Cazale in 1980 and met Frémon. Subsequently Grotowski asked Frémon to join the members of the Saint-Soleil group whom he had invited to work with him in Poland for eight months as part of the Theatre of Sources. Beside Frémon, 12 other Haitians went to Poland with Grotowski: Maud Robart, Jean-Claude 'Tiga' Garoute, Levey Exil, Veronique Jean, Pelazie Jeannot, Antilliome Richard, Saint Jean Saintjuste, Antoine Smith, Leane Smith, Phito Smith, Saint Jacques Smith and Stephen Smith (ibid.: 140).[13]

Frémon's role was different from that of the rest of the Saint-Soleil group. Bruno Chojak, currently the director of the Grotowski Institute's archive in Wrocław, and a participant in the Theatre of Sources, clearly remembers Frémon: 'As I remember it, he always steered clear from them [the Saint-Soleil group] and had completely separate activities, working as an individual with the European participants of the Theatre of Sources' (in ibid.: 142). Frémon's own identification as a Pole and his feeling of kinship with Poland is further evidenced in Chojak's testimony:

> Physically, he did not resemble the other Haitians whom Grotowski had brought along with him. Quite clearly, he did not belong to the cultist group [of Saint-Soleil], and he never failed to mention to every-one he was conversing with that he was a Pole, that 'we're all one fam-ily' (że jesteśmy jedną rodziną). It sounded very strange, but he surely felt even stranger, when he saw thousands of people of white skin all around him, and they were all supposed to be [. . .] Poles. His own concept of Poles was limited only to his own tribe in Haiti. He didn't know until that time for example, that Poland was not in Africa. [. . .] Such a consciousness would indicate at least, that he had never gone to school, he was authentically illiterate (in ibid.).

Frémon's expressed kinship with the Poles is not unlike the affinity that Grotowski articulated in relation to Haiti. Grotowski's interests in visiting Haiti were complex. However, his visit to Cazale was tied, according to Frémon's tes-timony documented by Pachoński and Wilson, to his search for his ancestors (1986: 316). Frémon considered himself to be the descendent of Blokowski-Detopski (i.e. Grotowski) who arrived to take him home to the land of his ancestors. This double-directionality of imagined ancestors and descendents situates both Grotowski and Frémon simultaneously in the position of ancestor and descendant. Both men look to each other for the source of at least part of their lineage. The two were both actively searching for the place and people of origin; both undertook journeys to the land(s) of their ancestors.[14]

The chronicle of the encounter between Frémon and Grotowski—itself multilayered, saturated by misconstructions and misapprehensions—challenges Grotowski's famous dictum 'You are someone's son.' To Grotowski's assertive definite, the narrative of Frémon and Grotowski answers with complexity and confusion. For whose sons are these two men, the Haitian houngan and the

Polish theatre director? They both look to each other in search of ancestors. Frémon's statements, in the various accounts, indicate that his sense of identification and belonging is self-defined. This, of course, does not negate the real genealogical link that he may have had to Poland. Frémon's identification with and sense of belonging to the Poland of Europe is imagined in Benedict Anderson's sense,[15] which, coincidentally, is the only sense in which Poland existed for a significant portion of its modern history. Poland's third partition went into effect on 24 October 1795 when the Polish-Lithuanian Commonwealth[16] was erased from the maps of Europe. From then until 1918, Poland existed as an imagined community, not a political fact. It was precisely at that historical juncture—at the end of the eighteenth century when Polish Legionnaires fought under foreign colours, in the hopes of one day re-establishing Poland as a political entity—that Poland existed only as an imagined community in the minds of those Poles who stayed in Haiti after it won its independence in 1804.

Frémon's insistence on his Polish identity and his sense of belonging ('we are all one family') in the face of experiencing radical cultural, linguistic and racial difference implies a greater regard for relational affinities than differences. However, that is not to say that he could not or did not experience a break or crisis of identity as a possible consequence of the culture shock that his presence in Poland may have spurred. However, the sources indicate that if there was a breach, it was resolved and that Frémon did not abandon his identification as a Pole, which he had prior to his journey there.

I would argue that for many Poles the notion of national identity is inextricably bound to race. In fact, it is racial (and not linguistic or cultural) difference that seems to come to the forefront when many Poles express discomfort with Frémon's self-identification as a Pole. This uneasiness is implicit not only in the remarks about the strangeness of the notion of a black Pole cited above, but also in the uncomfortable laughter which an account of Frémon's sentiments, recounted by Kolankiewicz, elicited in the mostly Polish audience at the talk given on the subject. This discomfort exposes an absolute rigidity of alignment of racial and national categories, at least in the dominant Polish imagination. The inability or unwillingness to imagine a nonwhite Pole that I read from the tension and uncomfortable laughter elicited by this notion in 2009 could only have been more intense during the early 1980s, when the borders of Poland were much more rigidly protected from the influx of foreigners.[17]

In contrast, Frémon's understanding of race and racial difference are more complex and fluid. Orizio's account frames Frémon's claims in the following manner:

'My father was whiter than your wife,' he said, glancing at Pia. 'But in Haiti a peasant always becomes black.' It was impossible to tell whether this was a reference to the climate or to the subtle sociological distinction between a *grand blanc*, or urban white, and a *petit blanc*, or peasant. 'If I spent a year in Poland I too would turn white. Now that I'm ill I'm black.' [. . .] 'You see, when I travel abroad I usually feel Polish, but here I'm Haitian. And now, at my age, with all the sun I've been exposed to, that is what I have become.' He raised his arm to show it to us and laughed bitterly. 'I'm Haitian even down to the colour of my skin' (2000: 145).

Without dismissing the possible interpretation of Frémon's statement as an attempt to map race along sociopolitical lines, I favour a more literal reading of his assertions. Frémon's claim to racial flux is inextricably tied to his own concept of self, skin colour included.[18]

A postcolonial critique, which might suggest that Frémon's association of blackness with low socioeconomic status, old age and sickness is indicative of an internalized abjection of his own race, while revealing partial factors at play, would nevertheless overlook his own agency. Moreover, such a critique imposes a postcolonial interpretive paradigm, which may have very little to do with the actual concerns, concepts and imagination of Frémon. I would argue that Frémon's notion of race is much more fluid than both the concept held by the Pole who cringes at the idea of a black Pole and the postcolonial critique, which might attack the premises of such racial discomfort. While the two might represent opposite sides of the spectrum, both stances are equally inflexible when trying to imagine a construction of race that is motile and not rigid. I propose taking Frémon's claim at face value to imagine a fluidity of his racial identification. That is not to say that race, in the sense of skin colour, is not fixed, but rather that Frémon's sense of self which he expresses in racial categories is not rigid and allows for movement across socially constructed racial boundaries.

The encounter between Grotowski and Frémon at the very least unsettles and complicates the hegemonic paradigms of the outsider/insider dichotomy. Moreover, it is significant in the context of the examination of transmission because it indicates a multidirectionality of lineage, or at least the social and personal construction of lineage.

Frémon's sense or construction of identity seems to place more emphasis on the affinities or identification with the other, in contrast to a paradigm of identity formation based on difference.[19] While, undoubtedly, identity formation is based on the negotiation of varied processes that may be plotted along a spectrum (which spans from a perception of sameness, similarity and affinity; identification with the other; imitation of the other; acknowledgement of difference; all the way to abjection), I maintain that in individual cases, emphasis is placed on only one aspect or step of this process. In the case of Amon Frémon, it appears that his insistence on identifying as a Pole (at least before his return to Haiti) and with Poles in the face of radical difference, which were probably articulated by (white) Poles through racial categories, seems to place greater value on the affinitive lines of identification. His stance expresses a more radical notion of race than the rigid posture that insists on the absolute concurrence of racial (white) and national (Polish) identity.

Grotowski's own stance vis-à-vis racial categories is not unlike Frémon's, in the sense that he sometimes identified himself with race(s) that are not his own by ordinary standards. By this I do not mean to imply that Grotowski, or Frémon for that matter, actually believed their skin had a colour other than what the world saw but, rather, that for them the process of identification was not limited to skin colour. In this regard, take Georges Banu's anecdote concerning the translation into French of Richards' *At Work with Grotowski on Physical Actions* (1999). Grotowski, famous for the care he took with linguistic expressions and his disregard for rules of grammar and proper language, insisted on a very specific, yet incorrect, French translation of a particular phrase. Banu, irritated by Grotowski's insistence, said: 'But Jerzy, this is the French of a *petit-nègre* [little nigger].' To which Grotowski retorted, 'But I am a *petit-nègre*' (Banu 2009). Whether Grotowski's response was a strategic identification intended to subvert the racism implicit in Banu's statement, or whether he actually identified with all of the various dimensions and tacit meanings implied by the notion of a *petit-nègre*, is impossible to tell. My contention is that it was a bit of both. However, what might be perceived as a fluctuating or fluid identification with racial categories including those other than one's 'own', is not unlike Frémon's flexible perception of self. Both Grotowski's identification with the *petit-nègre* as well as Frémon's identification as a Pole will elicit discomfort or critique, depending on the positioning of the viewer. However, it is this very stance of Frémon and Grotowski's shared notion of human relationality and belonging that disrupts the hegemonic colonial and postcolonial divide between outsider and insider.

It seems that obstacles to identification and belonging situated along racialized lines were not intrinsic to Frémon's or Grotowski's perception of themselves or their lineage. Beyond the connection that Grotowski drew between himself and Haiti, whether through real lineage or affective kinship, Grotowski's sense of ancestry was very broad and encompassed 'ancestors' to whom he could not draw any blood ties. For instance, in 'Tu es le fils de quelqu'un' Grotowski cites as his 'ancestor' not only the Polish Romantic poet Juliusz Słowacki (1809–49) but also the Madrid-born writer, poet and dramatist of the Spanish Golden Age, Pedro Calderón de la Barca (1600–81):

> In facing up to Calderon or Slowacki [*sic*] it was like the struggle between Jacob and the angel: 'Reveal unto me your secret!' But in actual fact, to hell with your secret. It's our secret that counts, we who are alive now. But if I know your secret, Calderon, then I can understand my own. I am not speaking to you as the writer whose work I must stage, I am speaking to you as a distant relation of mine. Which means that I'm speaking to my ancestors. And of course, I don't see eye-to-eye with my ancestors. But at the same time I cannot deny their existence. They are my base; they are my source. It's a personal question between me and them. So I have worked on dramatic literature and it's not by chance that they were almost always writers of the past: precisely because it had to do with ancestors, with other generations (1987a: 30).

Here, Grotowski positions the ancestor as a challenge—as someone we must rise to, in the search for our own truth, or our own 'secret', as he puts it. The imagined exchange with an ancestor is not the passing down of an unquestioned knowledge or wisdom, or its uncritical reception. Rather, what Grotowski describes is a dialogic encounter with the past personalized in the figure of an ancestor. The relationship with the ancestor is precisely that which ensures a creative growth or development on the part of the one searching, the 'descendent'. This is an affective relationship, which speaks to the most intimate needs and questions of the seeker.

In terms of the passage quoted above, Grotowski describes the intimate dialogic relationship established to an ancestor through the textual documents left behind, which in turn bear witness of the ancestor's own search. There is a relationship of questioning that is developed in relation to the cultural artefact of the text. It is this open-ended, inquiring nature of the relationship that makes it a living connection. In the context of the Theatre of Productions, Cieślak's performance of *The Constant Prince* is a clear example of this active and dialogic struggle-relationship with an ancestor. It is important to add that in no phase of Grotowski's lifelong research would he limit himself to a discourse with a single ancestor; there was always a multiplicity of interlocutors—dead and alive.

But it was not merely texts that constituted the material through which Grotowski and his collaborators established a dialogical and interrogatory relation to the past. In the same article, Grotowski describes the ways in which a traditional song, approached with a rigorous, questioning attitude, could reveal information about the concrete circumstances in which it was formed. Figured in such a manner the song serves as a connective tissue to the past, to one's ancestor, thereby providing insight into oneself. Grotowski speaks of the varied ways in which cultural artifacts, such as songs, are codified. He gives a generalized example of the way one can begin to discover how space is codified in a song:

People sing one way in the mountains and differently in the plains. In the mountains they sing from one high place to another, and the voice forms an arc: you gradually find the first incantations; you find the landscape. First there was this piece of wood, fire, animals, perhaps solitude: you began singing because you were afraid of being alone. Did you look for other people? Was it in the mountains? If it was in the mountains, were they on the other mountain? Who was the person who sang like this? Old or young? You finally discover that you come from somewhere, or as they traditionally say in an old French expression, 'Tu es le fils de quelqu'un' (You are someone's son). You aren't a tramp, you come from somewhere, from some country, from some place, from some landscape. There were identifiable people around you, near or far. It's you 200, 300, 400, or 1,000 years ago, but it's you, the same you. Because the person who began singing the first words was someone's son, from somewhere, from some place. So if you discover all this, you too are someone's son. If you don't you're not anyone's son; you are cut off, sterile, unproductive (ibid.: 40).

Productivity in this context is inextricably bound to a rootedness, to the process by which one becomes rooted. The actual place of origin, the source, the ancestor is imagined—not in a sense of fantasizing, however. The search is conducted actively with the body and the voice. The doing is an active questioning and, as Grotowski's description implies, is moored in the discovery of detail—the specificity of the context in which the song might have been sung in the past.

Grotowski believed that traditions are alive, that they can be contacted and re-lived as actual performed actions. Speaking at a Latin American Festival in Colombia in 1970, he stated:

> Tradition is truly active if it is like the air we breathe without thinking about it. If you must force yourself to accept tradition, if you must make spasmodic efforts to search for it and, having found it, to hold it up ostentatiously, then the tradition is no longer alive inside you. There is no point in doing that which has ceased to be alive because it will not be true (1972: 118).

Not only must tradition be tied to an active search in order to be alive, it also has to constitute a form of research. In this context, Grotowski referred to Gurdjieff's work on the Movements: [20]

> The Movements: they are something fundamental. Gurdjieff is rooted in a very ancient tradition, and at the same time he is contemporary. He knew, with a true competence, how to act in agreement with the modern world. It is a very rare case. In our times, all around these problems, there are so many attempts—easy, superficial, or simply sentimental. There, all at once appeared a person who brought a rigorous practice and a rigorous research. I mean it when I say research. For me, there is a very strong element of research. It is not like implanting a branch of the ancient tradition; it is also, on the same level, a deepened research which starts out from ancient elements, but which is, at

the same time, contemporary. After all, the traditions are only founded in this way (1997: 93).

Grotowski's description of Gurdjieff's approach is clearly also an apt reference to his own practice and understanding of tradition.

In his 'Untitled Text', Grotowski recounts a Tibetan Buddhist opinion, which contends that a 'tradition can live if the new generation goes a fifth ahead in respect to the preceding generation' (1999: 12). Richards expresses a fascination for the precision of this formula, which he sees both as a very serious and humorous articulation of the notion of tradition as research (2008: 152).

Jairo Cuesta, speaking about his work with Grotowski in Paratheatre and Theatre of Sources, describes how at one point in time Grotowski considered two different types of traditions side by side—the 'old traditions' and the *traditions nascens* (traditions being born, a new tradition):

> When you put a person who doesn't have a lot of knowledge of traditions [...] into the forest, this person begins to deal with intuitions, with his urges, with his dreams, with his energies [...]. And these energies, these intuitions, these old dreams start to talk to him, guiding him into something [...]. I think Grotowski was very interested to put his eyes on this kind of process. But at the same time, for him, it was very interesting to put his eyes onto something that is already happening: [...] how traditions work. For that reason in the Theatre of Sources it was important to put old traditions at the side of *traditions nascens*—traditions that are being born. I think for him it was important to see what the connection between the two of them was. And there are connections. There are very clear connections (in Dunkelberg 2008: 619).

According to Cuesta's testimony, Grotowski wanted to examine the two kinds of traditions alongside each other during this particular phase of research. However, Grotowski's later statements imply that the 'old traditions' and the *traditions nascens*, the traditions coming into life, were, in fact, fused together into one.

Grotowski's understanding of tradition as deep and active research, which starts out from ancient elements, dovetails with Barbara Kirshenblatt-Gimblett's notion of 'heritage' as a new mode of cultural production in the present that has recourse to the past (1998: 149). In both cases, the dead and obsolete come to life through a meaningful and meaning-making engagement with the past which takes place in the here and now. In fact, Kirshenblatt-Gimblett's argument that heritage is a way of producing 'hereness' (ibid.: 153), while made in an altogether different context, that of an analysis of the tourist industry, brings into unexpected focus Grotowski's praxis. Grotowski actually places tremendous emphasis on the awareness of the current moment and one's intense presence within it. Only by being entirely present—in the Buddhist phenomenological sense—can one access the deep past, the tradition.

This double directionality of attention holds taut the present and the past, the descendent and the ancestor. The discovery of the 'secret' of the ancestor or the past, leads to, or as I would argue, coincides with the discovery of one's own secret. It is my contention that this process of discovery of the self (descendent/present) and the other (ancestor/past) is simultaneous. This can be looked at along similar lines as the processes of individuation which, as I outlined above, can be schematized as being weighted differently. One process places greater emphasis on the discovery of self through the affinity, similarity and identification with the other. In another instance the dynamic of abjection may be more prevalent, and the discovery of self comes about as a result of the experience of difference (I know myself through that which I am not). Both processes invariably take place simultaneously, as one always encounters both similarity, affinity and difference in relation to other subjects and objects. Grotowski allows space for both paradigms. He formulates the self-discovery that takes place through difference as not seeing 'eye-to-eye' with the ancestor. Moreover, this is further expressed in Grotowski's defiant stance in regard to the past 'to hell with your secret'. While Grotowski acknowledges difference between the present and the past, the ancestor and descendent, and the existence of a personal 'secret' which does not necessarily coincide with the secrets of others, he does return to a notion of self-understanding through identification with the other.

While there may be a multiplicity of individual 'secrets' to be discovered, Grotowski believes that underlying all individual 'secrets' is a shared, or universal, secret. In fact, during the last phases of his research, Grotowski undertook a conscious effort to discover that universal 'secret', which he refers to as 'the essence.' As I discussed at more length in Chapter 1, the (re)discovery of essence is evidenced by the body of essence. It is, therefore, the active search, the *looking for* one's ancestor that creates a meaningful connection between the descendent or doer and her ancestor.

Grotowski's invitation quoted by Frémon, 'Let me take you to the land of your ancestors' (in Thomson 1992: 54–5) extends more broadly and takes on a larger significance when examined in relation to the latter phases of his work. From the time of the Theatre of Sources Grotowski invites and guides his collaborators to the land of their ancestors. The direct connection that is established between the descendent and ancestor in the latter three phases of Grotowski's practical work is a line to the origin or source. This is also a practical investigation into the nature of the self, on which Grotowski embarked early in his life:

> [F]rom this time on I started to try, practically, to make this investiga-
> tion: 'Who-am-I?' which was not a mental investigation, but rather as
> if going more and more towards the source from which this feeling of
> 'I' appears. The more this source seems to be approached, the less the
> 'I' is. It is as if a river would turn and flow towards its source. And in
> the source, there is no longer a river? (2001b: 254–5).

The connective line to the ancestor as source is one that is direct and personal, discovered through practical investigation within the work itself. The discovery of essence in the ancestor coincides with the discovery of essence within oneself.[21]

Alongside the relationality with an ancestor described above, starting with the Theatre of Sources, the process of direct transmission from one person to another becomes central. Actually, Grotowski's interest in direct transmission began long before he invited master teachers from various traditions to transmit their embodied knowledge of performative techniques within the framework of his research. In a 1995 interview with Thibaudat, Grotowski states:

> Since childhood I have been interested in different kinds of 'psy-
> chophysical' techniques. In fact, since the age of nine, my first points
> of orientation have been the great figures of Hindu techniques. And
> this first center of interest (how to work on oneself with someone else,
> in a performative context, so to speak) subsequently passed through
> theatre. In the course of my life I have always looked for contact with
> people who were in unbroken connection with this or that technique

and tradition. And there, in different fields, I have received a direct transmission (in Thibaudat 1995: 31).

As I have already demonstrated, Grotowski construed ancestral relations very broadly; he did not limit lineage to genealogical descent. When considering the connections which Grotowski actively made with various traditions, it is perhaps more apt to think of a web than a single strand.

Moreover, Grotowski's notion of the cradle of Western civilization is very broadly construed. He speaks of 'some large "cradle of tradition", including ancient Egypt, the land of Israel, Greece, and ancient Syria as the cradle of the Occident' (Richards 2008: 38). This conceptualization places the performative techniques of the African diaspora within the realm of Western heritage. Therefore, it would not have been a stretch for him to think of himself as a descendent of this particular line of transmission. The specific line of Afro-Haitian songs, which Grotowski 'intuitively' traced back to a very ancient line of African songs (ibid.), along with the ritual movements associated with the Haitian *yanvalou*, came to constitute the core performative elements or tools used in the Art as vehicle phase. This line continues to be a vital resource in the work of the Workcenter of Jerzy Grotowski and Thomas Richards.

While Grotowski drew or stole, as he liked to say, from various traditions, here I will examine more closely only one strand of transmission, that of Afro-Haitian song and ritual movement. I have already traced Grotowski's familial connection to Haiti, whether real or imagined. In what follows, I will consider his actual journeys to Haiti.

Grotowski first travelled to Haiti in 1977, where he met the ethnologist Louis Mars in Port-au-Prince.[22] Grotowski returned to Haiti the following year when he gave an eight-hour talk on Paratheatre at the L'Institut Francais d'Haiti (Dunkelberg 2008: 603). It was also in 1978 that Grotowski first worked with the Saint-Soleil community in their mountain base between 27 November and 5 December 1978 (ibid.). In May 1979, Grotowski returned to Haiti to prepare for the Theatre of Sources project, which took place from 18 July to 8 August 1979. For this project, Grotowski was accompanied by an international team of Zbigniew 'Téo' Spychalski (Poland), Dominique Gerard (France), François Kahn (France), Elizabeth Havard (USA), Jairo Cuesta (Colombia) and Stefano Vercelli (Italy) (ibid.: 614).

As in other sites in which Theatre of Sources took place, the working group in Haiti was comprised of Grotowski's group, theatre students or artists from local urban centres and people from traditional villages (ibid.: 600). In Haiti, participants also included members of the Saint-Soleil community, as well as the traditional Vodou practitioners Micado and Eliezer Cadet and the houngan Amon Frémon.

The Cadets were exceptional because they were the only people from a Theatre of Sources host country who later joined Grotowski on his expeditions outside Poland. Eliezer Cadet was Grotowski's sole companion on his trip to Nigeria in August 1979 and Micado Cadet accompanied Grotowski to India in February 1980 (ibid.: 599).

Saint-Soleil was cofounded in 1974 by Jean-Claude 'Tiga' Garoute and Maud Robart in Soissons-la-Montagne, near Port-au-Prince. It was an artist collective that became known internationally through André Malraux's book *La Metamorphose de Dieux: L'Intemporel* (1976), as well as through Jean-Marie Drot's film documenting Malraux's visit to Haiti. Tiga and Robart purchased land in the mountains and distributed art supplies to peasants who possessed no formal training. Robart describes the activities of Saint-Soleil:

> Tiga's method consisted of giving the artists no technical advice at all in order to allow them to become aware, on their own, of the act of creation, each according to his own rhythm and through totally free expression. [. . .] The country people realized these works at home, outside of their professional activities. They made a habit of holding artist meetings. Very often these meetings ended with tales, stories, legends, and traditional songs. That is how the theater of Saint-Soleil was born in Soisson la Montagne (in Dunkelberg 2008: 601–2).

Tiga and Robart were not traditional practitioners of Vodou but came instead from the Haitian urban upper class.[23] Despite this, Saint-Soleil's search for the sources of creativity in artistic expression also drew on the song and dance practices associated with Vodou (ibid.: 602).

Cuesta's account of his work in Haiti reveals that Grotowski was also involved with the work on a practical level, learning directly from a houngan: 'When I was in Haiti, I had a very important meeting with one of the great priests from the voudoun religion, that was one of the masters or the teachers of Tiga and Maude. He was a very, very strong person [. . .] We began to work Grotowski, him and me [on] rituals of fire' (in ibid.: 610).

What is important to note here is that while the culture of Vodou was undoubtedly in the backdrop of their childhood landscape in Haiti, both Tiga and Robart were not acculturated into the traditional practices of Vodou as young children, but came to the practice through a conscious choice as adults. Moreover, Robart became interested and began to (re)discover traditional Haitian practices through her French husband, a professor who travelled through Haiti:

> Beginning in 1966, she [Robart] discovered her native country through numerous expeditions organized by her husband Guy Robart, a French professor in the Natural Sciences, across the wildest [*plus sauvages*] regions of the country. These expeditions gave her the possibility to get in touch with the most enigmatic and unknown aspects of popular culture in Haiti (Robart 2009).[24]

In 1983–84 Tiga and Robart worked with Grotowski during the Objective Drama programme in UC Irvine, California. After that, Robart intermittently collaborated with Grotowski and worked as a master teacher at the Workcenter in Pontedera until 1993.

Richards worked closely with Tiga and Robart, beginning in the Objective Drama programme. Richards recalls that when he first heard the traditional songs of Haiti it was as if he were hearing the voice of his grandmother, which touched something deep inside of him that had not been touched up to that point (Richards 2008: 2). Richards' paternal line comes from the Caribbean. His grandmother is from Jamaica. Richards had already learned African, West African and Caribbean songs from a West African practitioner and other sources before coming to work with Grotowski (ibid.: 42). Subsequently, he learnt Afro-Haitian songs and movements from Tiga and Robart, primarily through oral and embodied transmission. This direct transmission of songs was extremely important in the work. However, Richards differentiates this process of learning from the type of transmission that takes place in a culture in which there is a 'tradition that is living' (ibid.). In that context, the transmission process takes place over an extended period of time and produces a gradual but deep immersion: 'So even before the child begins to sing, the songs are deeply incorporated into its body, and also resonating within, in its being' (ibid.: 43).

The importance of learning Afro-Haitian songs from a living voice is further emphasized in Wolford Wylam's recollection of her work with Robart in the Objective Drama programme in 1989: 'Participants who asked to audiotape Robart's songs were denied. Tape recording, we were instructed, cannot capture the vibratory pattern, the subtle energy of a song; only through direct interaction between teacher and novice can such knowledge be conveyed' (Wolford 1996: 41).

However, Grotowski's openness and refusal to circumscribe himself within a fixed system is evidenced in the following incident narrated by Richards:

> One day, in the beginning of my apprenticeship when we were already in Italy, we were talking in his [Grotowski's] house. We had been analyzing the fact that something was blocking me in my process related to the songs. And as I went to the bathroom, I began to sing softly on my way. It was an African melody, this time one that I had learned from an ethnological record! Just from a record! Grotowski suddenly called from the kitchen, 'Stop, stop! Come back! What were you just singing? There was something special in your sonic vibration. What was that?' I said what it was and how I learned it. Much to my surprise he said, 'Let's go to work.' I said, 'But . . . it's not orthodox, I just learned it from a record.' He said quietly, 'Please Thomas . . . don't be ashamed' (2008: 44).

Grotowski's 'unorthodox' approach, in which he allows space to subvert his own previously established modus operandi, destabilizes romanticized notions of 'authentic' oral transmission. Another important point made by Richards is that oral transmission does not guarantee that a 'true oral transmission' is being passed or received. The quality of one's capacity of doing and the integrity of work is not ensured by the fact that the transmission is oral (ibid.: 43). The key in distinguishing the efficacy of oral or embodied transmission, according to Richards, is whether through the work one awakens or remains asleep (ibid.).

One of the intentions of Grotowski's work with traditional performative techniques was to isolate particular elements that could serve as tools for work on 'inner action' which, in Grotowski's opinion, would have an objective effect on the doer irrespective of her or his culture or race. Richards speaks cogently about the objective nature of the potential effect that the songs may have on a doer:

> What's possible through the work with and around these songs is appealing to the human being—appealing meaning calling something in the human being, allowing some process in the human being— rather than someone of a particular nationality, race, or sex. It's evident to me from the practical research we've done that the objective impact of the proper work on and around such a song can be the same on persons from different cultures (ibid.: 39).

Not only does the proper use of these traditional instruments have comparable effects on doers, 'underneath and between every deep and alive tradition is something technically similar' (ibid.: 41).

While Richards learnt the traditional techniques from those who can arguably be called masters of the Haitian tradition—although, as noted earlier, both these practitioners came to the work as adults and were not exposed to the performative techniques through a gradual immersive process as children— he states that he learned the 'inner action' from no one else but Grotowski himself:

> I happened to find the way to reconnect to my so-called African line of tradition from a Polish man with a white beard, in California and Italy. It seems absurd, but it's working. Grotowski had worked with practitioners from the African-Caribbean tradition, and not only from that tradition. He worked in depth with practitioners from many cultures. And then he looked, really, to transmit what he knew, practically, not just theoretically, and not in an easy way (ibid.: 40).

Richards' description of the quality of silence that Grotowski exhibited at conferences, which was the result of a high level of concentration and which in turn elicited a rare quality of attention in the listener, points to one of the key elements of transmission. Beside the importance of the content of the words themselves, it was the quality of attention—which mobilized and activated the listener—that was transmitted.

Notes

1 All translations from this source are mine.

2   Cap Français, present-day Cap-Haïtien, is located on the north coast of Haiti.

3   The Polish Legions were special Polish military units serving the French army from the 1790s to the 1810s. Also known as the Polish army in exile, the Polish units were created with the help of Napoleon Bonaparte during the third partition of Poland (1795). The Legions were formed under the tutelage of Polish revolutionaries such as Tadeusz Kościuszko, Henryk Dąbrowski, Karol Kniaziewicz and Józef Wybicki. The Polish Legionnaires served under the French colours in the hopes that revolutionary France would eventually come to Poland's aid against its partitioners, which at the time were also France's enemies: Prussia, Austria and Imperial Russia.

4   St Domingue or Saint-Domingue was the name of the French colony in the Caribbean from 1659 until 1804, when it became the independent nation of Haiti. Saint-Domingue is the French version of Santo Domingo or San Domingo, the name given by the Spanish colonialists prior to the French control of the island. Santo Domingo alternated with Hispaniola (present-day Haiti and the Dominican Republic), the Latinized version of La Española, the name given by Christopher Columbus, who took possession of the island on 5 December 1492. Prior to the arrival of the Spanish, the island was inhabited by the Arawak, Carib and Taíno people. There were various indigenous names which circulated prior to Spanish contact, among them *Haiti*, meaning 'mountainous land', used by the Taíno to refer to the island or its western parts. Officially known as the Republic of Haiti, the island's Creole Haitian name is Ayiti.

5   The slave rebellion of St Domingue was initiated at a religious ceremony held at Bois Caïman on 14 August 1791 by Dutty Boukman, a houngan (Vodou priest) and maroon leader. In August 1793, a French commissioner was forced to free the slaves in his jurisdiction in order to prevent military disaster. In 1794 the French National Convention formally abolished slavery and granted civil and political rights to all black men in the colonies. However, in 1801 Bonaparte sent a large expeditionary force led by Leclerc to St Domingue with secret instructions to restore slavery.

6   For a detailed historical account of the Polish presence in Haiti, see Pachoński and Wilson's *Poland's Caribbean Tragedy* (1986) and Rypson's *Being Poloné in Haiti* (2008).

7   Scylla was a black commander. 'Congos' was the name given to the most recent arrivals from Africa, 'who quickly established tribal affiliations and were led by houngans' (Pachoński and Wilson 1986: 59).

8   If one considers Haiti Grotowski's second homeland, it is certainly not the last. Grotowski had a deep connection to other places, most notably India, which he visited on numerous occasions, and which was the place of his famous and most dramatic psychophysical transformation. According to Osiński, Haiti was Grotowski's 'third "homeland of the heart" (*ojczyzna serdeczna*), Poland and India being the other two "heartfelt homelands"' (in Rypson 2008: 141).

9   Zbigniew Osiński claims that there is, in fact, a blood relation between Jerzy and Feliks Grotowski.

10 Kermit Dunkelberg traces Grotowski's interest in Haiti back to his encounter with Jean-Marie Drot, a French film director during the Laboratory Theatre's appearance at the Theatre of Nations Festival in 1966. Drot had a strong interest in Haiti and encouraged Grotowski to travel there (Dunkelberg 2008: 601).

11 Amon Frémont is an alternate spelling of the houngan's name.

12 During the period of martial law in Poland (13 December 1981 to 22 July 1983) a curfew was imposed.

13 Sebastian Rypson cites his private correspondence with Leszek Kolankiewicz as the source of this information. Kermit Dunkelberg maintains that Micado and Eliezer Cadet also travelled to Poland with Grotowski (2008: 599). The source of his claim is Robert Różycki's compilation of information from Kolankiewicz's 1986 University of Warsaw dissertation 'Poszukiwania etnologiczne wspóczesnej awangardy teatralnej' [Ethnological research of the contemporary theatrical avantgarde] for publication in *Notatnik Teatralny* (Różycki 1992).

14 In *With Jerzy Grotowski, Nienadówka*, Jill Godmilow *documents* Grotowski's return to the village in eastern Poland where he lived during the war. His journey to Cazale is a variation on this theme of his search for his own sources, which he conceived not as a singular source but one of multiple syncretic origins.

15 In his work *Imagined Communities* (1983), Benedict Anderson argues that communities and nations are socially constructed, perceived by people who imagine themselves as a group.

16 The Polish-Lithuanian Commonwealth, also known as the First Polish Republic (Pierwsza Rzeczpospolita or Rzeczpospolita Obojga Narodów), was formed in 1569 through the consolidation of the Kingdom of Poland and the Grand Duchy of Lithuania. In the sixteenth and seventeenth centuries, it was the largest and most populated nation in Europe. The Commonwealth not only covered the former territories of Poland and Lithuania, but also included the entire region of Belarus and

Latvia, large parts of the Ukraine and Estonia, as well as part of present-day western Russia.

17 In addition to the dearth of influx of racially and ethnically diverse peoples into Poland, Polish mentality had long been shaped by the careful cultivation of Polish nationalism, which excluded all internal cultural, racial and linguistic difference. Beyond the erasure of the history of the pre–Second World War Jewish presence in Poland, other minority groups had been systematically excluded from the concept of Polish national identity. In fact, I would argue that the construction of a monolithic Polish identity depended on the systematic exclusion of minority groups such as the Tatars, Lemkos, Kashubs (Kashubians), Roma and Armenians, among others.

18 It should be stated, in the context of this discussion, that while the categories deployed by Frémon are national and racial, there is a high probability that his understanding of the terms is quite different from the ways in which they are conceived in contemporary popular imaginaries. Moreover, Frémon's understanding of Polishness and what it means to identify as a Pole are undoubtedly very different from what these same terms might mean for someone living in Poland. I would speculate that the terms of racial difference came to the fore at the time of Frémon's visit to Poland, where the category of racial difference became that which barred him from being recognized as a Pole by (white) Poles.

19 One such theory of individuation that is premised on difference is Julia Kristeva's notion of abjection as an identity-forming process, in which identity is construed through the rejection of that which 'I' am not (1980).

20 Gurdjieff's Movements are sacred dances and esoteric movements based on a repertoire of ancient traditional dances that he learned during his travels in the Near East, Middle East and Asia. The Movements constitute a form of embodied knowledge with each movement corresponding to and representing a cosmic truth that can be read by the initiate.

21 Dunkelberg draws attention to another more pragmatically anchored sense of 'source' or 'origin', contrasting it to the more rhetorical sweep of Grotowski's discussions of Theatre of Sources. In this sense the origin is the moment of the birth of the organic impulse in the body in the here and now (2008: 618).

22 For a discussion of the relationship of Mars' concept of 'ethnodrama' and Grotowski's work see Dunkelberg (2008: 603–18).

23 While Vodou is the religion of the vast majority of Haitians, the middle and upper classes, for the most part, do not practise as a result of the influence of conventional

Euro-American criteria of what constitutes 'civilized' behaviour as well as pressure exerted by the Catholic Church.

24 All translations from this source are mine.

EPILOGUE

In a chapter of *Towards a Poor Theatre* entitled 'He Wasn't Entirely Himself', Grotowski conducts a critical analysis of Antonin Artaud in which he tries to strip Artaud down to his bare essence. Grotowski argues that Artaud's misfortune lies in the fact that his sickness was misaligned with the sickness of civilization. Grotowski takes Artaud's self-diagnosis articulated in a letter to Jacques Rivière—'I am not entirely myself'—as the quintessential definition of his dilemma (Grotowski 1969: 91). Grotowski writes about Artaud: 'He was not merely himself, he was someone else. He grasped half of his own dilemma: how to be oneself. He left the other half untouched: how to be whole, how to be complete' (ibid.). The double meaning of the notion 'He was not entirely himself' encapsulates the theme of this book. Grotowski's own concept of self was not that of a discrete entity but, rather, as a relational being who becomes fully oneself only through and in relation to the other. This process takes place not only through the dialogical relationship with an (imagined) ancestor, as discussed in Chapter 4, but also through a being together with another human being in the here and now. For Grotowski, the *via negativa* applied internally is a mode of doing which arrives 'to the being that [one] is, [. . .] only through a being other than I' (1979b).

The epigraph that stands at the beginning of this book is a call to 'cross the boundaries with your whole being, with honesty, discipline and precision' (ibid.). This challenge I read as yet another variation of this notion of the porous nature of self, which carries multiple meanings. First and foremost it encapsulates Grotowski's challenge to cross one's own boundaries, to go beyond the limits imposed by the individual and society—the inherited ideas that proscribe what is possible for the individual. Beyond this, however, and in light of the foregoing study, I read implicit in this statement a call to cross boundaries of one's individuated being by transcending the self through relationality with the other. The notion of the porousness and connectedness of self in relation to the other is articulated by Richards:

> I remember flying back one time to Italy after Christmas holidays, which I had spent in New York. On the plane next to me there was a young Hasid who was praying throughout the flight. I was deeply

interested in his process, and as the flight progressed some unspoken connection grew between us. In one moment, out of the blue, he turned to me and quietly said, 'I am blessed if you find what you are looking for.' These were the only words that passed between us on that flight. I was struck by the wisdom behind those words. He would be blessed if I found what I was looking for. The whole concept of what was 'his' and what was 'mine' blurred. Where did *his* experience, *my* experience begin and end? I was struck by the lack of possessiveness and the well wishing behind those words (2008: 156; emphasis in original).

Richards' anecdote clearly illustrates the I-I concept that Grotowski articulated during the Art as vehicle phase of research.

It is in the work on I-I that there is an absolute coincidence of the ends and means. I extend myself, cross the limits of my self, through the other, through and with my *bliźni*, my 'Twin', my brother, to realize fully my own being. The concurrance of being oneself (*być sobą*) and being whole, complete (*być całym, całkowitym*) is at the heart of Grotowski's praxis in which self-realization is extricably tied to the process of self-discovery undertaken by Performer conceived as *człowiek poznania* (man of knowledge). To be yourself is to be something *more* than yourself, whether it is your (imagined) anscestor, the person next to you or what Grotowski at times articulated as the 'higher connection'.

Grotowski's notion of the self is expansive and extends beyond the ordinary and discrete 'I' of everyday life. Grotowski's I-I encompasses those who came before and the bliźni in the here and now. Moreover, it contains the notion of an internal I-I which, as discussed in chapters 1 and 3, Grotowski designates as a silent and immobile gaze of another part of the self, a witness, perceived as existing outside of time. It is the development of the I-I that opens up the potential for self-realization or what in later phases of research was formulated by Grotowski as the *body as essence*.

While the coming into (one's own) being through the other is at the heart of the Grotowski work, its realization is complex and multifaceted. Coming into being involves the (re)discovery of essence through the process of active remembering; the exploration of vigilance understood as enhanced states of awareness and an active wakefulness that lead to acts of witnessing and testification; the vertically structured work on the refinement of energies; and, finally, the numerous and complex lines of transmission conceived as a multidirectional process of relationality with the (imagined) ancestor to the broadly construed 'twin'.

The interrelatedness of these various aspects of his work are articulated most fully by Grotowski:

[W]e must hold on to our quality of man which, in numerous traditional languages, is connected with the vertical axis, 'to stand'. (In certain languages the word for man is 'that which stands'.) The term 'axial
man' is used in modern psychology. There's something that watches,
that keeps watch, there's a quantity of vigilance, of watching. In the
Bible, as well as in the Gospels, we often come across the expression,
'Be vigilant! Be vigilant!' Observe what happens. Reptile brain or reptile body, it's your animal, yours, but be a man! Watch what is happening. Watch over yourself. Then it's as if there were the presence of the
register of instinct and that of consciousness, at the two extremities of
the same register. Normally, our daily lukewarm existence leaves us
somewhere between the two, neither fully animal nor fully human. We
move confusedly between the two. But in authentic traditional techniques as well as in every true performing art, we hold on to the two
extremes simultaneously. At the beginning you stand upright. The
beginning consists of everything that is your original nature, present
here, now, your original nature with all its divine and animal aspects
at the same time, instincts and passions. But at the same time you must
be vigilant with your consciousness. The more you are in your beginning, the more you must 'stand upright.' It is this watchful consciousness which makes a man of you. It's something very exact and it's
precisely this tension between the two extremities which creates a con-
tradictory and mysterious fullness (1987a: 37–8).

In this volume I have undertaken the project of exploring the points of contact among memory, vigilance, witnessing, verticality and transmission from various phases of Grotowski's research in order to begin to approach the totality of his complex understanding of self-development between self and other. I examine the Grotowski work on its own terms. The complexity of such a project becomes even more compounded when one considers that, for rea-sons explained in the preface and introduction, the borders between that which is *mine* and which is *Grotowski's* are neither clear nor stable.

The nature of this study diverges from Grotowski's own modus operandi, which was invariably rooted in practice. Grotowski's practice grew intuitively and organically—to borrow Grotowski's term—from the needs of the people involved in the work, and *only later* was synthesized and articulated in talks which were subsequently edited into texts. For him, practice preceded and superseded theory. The themes and distillations that emerged from Grotowski's practice, some of which I have treated at length here, are impossible to either 'prove' or 'disprove' on a theoretical level.

Work that would truly put to task Grotowski's assertions is impossible without long-term practical research. However productive and interesting my, or any other, theoretical analyses might prove, Grotowski can only be answered on a practical level; or, at the very least, through work that involves a constant movement between or synthesis of the practical and theoretical.

Grotowski's long-term, rigorous practical work is an important paradigm of embodied research which—despite its deep investment in 'the body' and various notions of embodiment—continues to offer a rich area of inquiry within the field of performance studies. As an active area of research and questioning conducted with the body-being of the doer, the Grotowski work is the literalization and concretization of the highly theoretical and often abstract discussions of one of the main areas of performance studies—embodied practice as a way of knowing.

Beyond providing an alternate methodological paradigm of research, Grotowski's work implies something much more radical. His work is a 'conscious and deliberate blurring of the sense of self' (Richards 2010). It is a concrete and literal work intended to blur the boundaries between self and other. The underlying assumption of the work is that the self does not end at the limits of the body, but extends beyond it into a larger field that surrounds the body. This notion makes itself manifest in the practical work of the Workcenter through the emphasis on the development of a perception or sensitivity to the energetic field surrounding the body. Richards alludes to the possibility *of being inside the other* while maintaining physical distance (ibid.). It is this conscious, deliberate and literal unsettling of the boundaries between the self and other that holds the most radical social, political and theoretical implications.

Where are our boundaries? And where are the boundaries of the Sun?

We look: it is a vibrating sphere from which perturbations emanate, explosions, sun storms, expansions. And we think that these are more or less its boundaries. But these are not the boundaries of the solar body. Because astronomers speak of 'solar wind'. What is this wind? These are corpuscles of solar matter emanating far into our planetary system and forming a type of web, which surrounds the entire system protecting it from external cosmic rays. Is this the boundary of the Sun? Perhaps. But if so we are in the Sun. The same is true of our body (Grotowski 1979a: 96).

REFERENCES

AHRNE, Marianne (director). 1993. *Il Teatr Laboratorium di Jerzy Grotowski* (The laboratory of Jerzy Grotowski). RAI (Radiotelevisione Italiana S.p.A.). DVD.

———. 2009. 'From the Film *Il Teatr Laboratorium di Jerzy Grotowski*: Jerzy Grotowski Interviewed by Marianne Ahrne' (Mario Biagini trans.) in Paul Allain (ed.), *Grotowski's Empty Room*. London: Seagull Books, pp. 219–28.

ANDERSON, Benedict 1983. *Imagined Communities: Reflections on the Origin and Spread of Nationalism*. London: Verso.

ATTISANI, Antonio. 2008. 'Acta Gnosis' (Elisa Poggelli trans.). *TDR* 52(2): 75–106.

BANU, Georges. 2009. 'Stanislavski/Meyerhold et Brook/Grotowski: Le Sens de ces amitiés dans le XX ème siècle' (Stanislavski/Meyerhold and Brook/Grotowski: The Meaning of These Friendships in the Twentieth Century). Talk given at the Year of Grotowski Inauguration, Wrocław, Poland, 13 January.

BAUMRIN, Seth. 2009. 'Ketmanship in Opole: Jerzy Grotowski and the Price of Artistic Freedom'. *TDR* 53(4): 49–77.

BENEDETTI, Jean. 1998. *Stanislavski and the Actor*. New York: Routledge.

———. 2004 [1982]. *Stanislavski: An Introduction*. New York: Routledge.

BENJAMIN, Jonathan, Richard Ebstein and Robert H. Belmaker. 2002. *Molecular Genetics and the Human Personality*. Washington, DC: American Psychological Association Press.

BIAGINI, Mario. 2008. 'Meeting at La Sapienza; or, On the Cultivation of Onions' (Lisa Wolford Wylam trans.). *TDR* 52(2): 150–77.

———. 2010. Personal conversation with author, New York, NY, 2 January.

BONARSKI, Andrzej. 1979. 'Rozmowa z Grotowskim' (Conversation with Grotowski). *Ziarno* (Seed). Warsaw: Czytelnik, 19–44.

BROOK, Peter. 2009. 'Introduction to the Film *Akropolis*' in Georges Banu and Grzegorz Ziółkowski with Paul Allain (eds), *With Grotowski: Theatre Is Just a Form*. Wrocław: The Grotowski Institute, pp. 14–24.

BRUNTON, Paul. 1939. *Ścieżkami jogów* (A Search in Secret India) (Wanda Dynowska trans.). Lwów: Książnica-Atlas.

BUBER, Martin. 1958. *I and Thou*, 2nd EDN. New York: Scribner.

BURZYŃSKI, Tadeusz, and Zbigniew Osiński. 1979. *Grotowski's Laboratory*. Warsaw: Interpress.

CARNICKE, Sharon Marie. 2009. *Stanislavsky in Focus: An Acting Master for the Twenty-First Century*. London: Routledge.

CASHMAN, Daniel E. 'Grotowski: His Twentieth Anniversary'. *Theatre Journal* 31(4): 440–6.

CIEŚLAK, Ryszard, Jerzy Grotowski and Max Waldman. 1970. '*The Constant Prince*'. *TDR* 14(2): 164–77.

DUNKELBERG, Kermit. 2008. 'Grotowski and North American Theatre: Translation, Transmission, Dissemination'. PhD diss., New York University.

ELIADE, Mircea. 1984. *Yoga: Nieśmiertelność i wolność* (Yoga: Immortality and Freedom) (Bolesław Baranowski trans.). Warsaw: Państwowe Wydawnictwo Naukowe.

FISCHER, Adam. 1921. *Zwyczaje pogrzebowe ludu polskiego* (Funerary Customs of the Polish Nation). Lwów: Nakładem Zakładu Narodowego im. Ossolińskich.

FLASZEN, Ludwik. 1957. 'Klapa, albo o potrzebie radości' (A Flop, or On the Need for Joy). *Przegląd Kulturalny* 33 (15–21 August): 1, 5.

———. 1958. *Głowa i mur* (Head and Wall). Kraków: Wydawnictwo Literackie.

———. 2006. 'Komentarze Ludwika Flaszena' (Ludwik Flaszen's Commentary) in Janusz Degler and Grzegorz Ziółkowski (eds), *Misterium zgrozy i urzeczenia: Przedstawienia Jerzego Grotowskiego i Teatru Laboratorium* (Mysterium Tremendum et Fascinans. The Performances of Jerzy Grotowski and the Laboratory Theatre). Wrocław: Instytut im. Jerzego Grotowskiego, pp. 27–97.

FUMAROLI, Marc. 2009. 'Grotowski, Or the Border Ferryman' in Paul Allain (ed.), *Grotowski's Empty Room*. London: Seagull Books, pp. 195–215.

GODMILOW, Jill (director). 1980. *With Jerzy Grotowski, Nienadówka, 1980*. Facets. DVD.

———. 1981. *The Vigil*. Atlas Theatre Company. DVD.

GOLDMANN, Arthur. 1926. 'Di Vakhnakht Bay Viner Yidn onheyb 15tn Yorhundret' (The Vakhnaht of the Jews of Vienna in the Fifteenth Century) in *Landoy-bukh: Dr. Alfred Landoy tsu zayn 75stn geboyrnstag dem 25stn November 1925* (Jubilee Volume for Dr. Alfred Landoy on his 75th birthday on the 25th of November 1925). Vilne: Vilner Farlag fun B. Kletskin, pp. 91–4.

GRONDIN, Michael W. 2002. *Grondin's Interlinear Coptic/English Translation of The Gospel of Thomas*. Available at http://gospel-thomas.net/gtbypage_112702.pdf. (last accessed on 5 August 2013).

GROTOWSKI, Jerzy. 1955a. 'Czerwony Balonik'(The Little Red Balloon). Od A do Z (supplement), *Dziennik Polski* 1, 1–2 January. p. 2.

———. 1955b. 'W tonacji entuzjastycznej'(In an Enthusiastic Tone). *Dziennik Polski* 27, 1 February. pp. 2–3.

———. 1957. 'Co Dalej' (What's Next). *Walka Młodych* (Katowice), 1 April. pp. 3–5.

———. 1969. *Towards a Poor Theatre* (Eugenio Barba ed.). London: Methuen.

———. 1972. 'Co było. (Kolumbia—lato 1970. Festiwal Ameryki Łacińskiej)' (What was. Columbia—summer 1970. Latin American festival). *Dialog* 10: 111–18.

———. 1973. 'Holiday: The Day That Is Holy' (Bolesław Taborski trans.). *TDR* 17(2): 113–35.

———. 1975. 'Przesięwzięcie Góra—Project: The Mountain of Flame'. *Odra* 6: 23–7.

———.1979a. 'Działanie jest dosłowne' (Action is Literal). *Dialog* 9: 95–101.

———. 1979b. 'Ćwiczenia' (Exercises). *Dialog* 12: 12–137.

———. 1987a. 'Tu es le fils de quelqu'un' (You Are Someone's Son) (Ronald Packham ed. and Jacques Chwat trans.). *TDR* 31(3): 30–41.

———. 1987b. 'Teatr Źródeł' (Theatre of Sources). *Zeszyty Literackie* 19 (Summer): 102–15.

———. 1992. '*Le Prince constant* de Ryszard Cieslak' in Georges Banu (ed.), *Ryszard Cieślak, acteur-emblème des années soixante* (Ryszard Cieślak, Actor-Emblem of the Sixties). Arles: Actes Sud Papiers, pp. 13–21.

———. 1995a. 'From the Theatre Company to Art as vehicle' in Thomas Richards, *At Work with Grotowski on Physical Actions*. London: Routledge, pp. 115–35

———.1995b. *Titres et Travaux* (Titles and Works). Unpublished.

———. 1997. 'A Kind of Volcano: An Interview with Jerzy Grotowski' in Jacob Needleman and George Baker (eds), *Gurdjieff: Essays and Reflections on the Man and His Teaching*. New York: Continuum, pp. 87–106.

———. 1999. 'Untitled Text by Jerzy Grotowski, Signed in Pontedera, Italy, 4 July 1998' (Mario Biagini trans.). *TDR* 43(2): 11–12.

———. 2001a. 'Performer' in Richard Schechner and Lisa Wolford (eds), *The Grotowski Sourcebook*. London: Routledge, pp. 376–80.

———. 2001b. 'Theatre of Sources' in Richard Schechner and Lisa Wolford (eds), *The Grotowski Sourcebook*. London: Routledge, pp. 252–70.

GROTOWSKI, Kazimierz. 2001. 'Podróż w biografię: Spotkanie z Kazimierzem Grotowskim, 17 października 1999' (A Journey into Biography: A Meeting with Kazimierz Grotowski, November 17, 1999). *Notatnik Teatralny* 22–23: 8–25.

HOUTSMA, M. T. 1987. *E. J. Brill's First Encyclopaedia of Islam, 1913–1936*. Leiden: E. J. Brill.

JANOWSKI, Mieczysław. 2010. Telephone conversation with author, New York. 9 March.

KELERA, Józef. 1965. 'Teatr w stanie łaski' (Theatre in a State of Grace). *Odra* 11: 71–4.

KIRSHENBLATT-GIMBLETT, Barbara. 1998. *Destination Culture: Tourism, Museums, and Heritage*. Berkeley: University of California Press.

KOLANKIEWICZ, Leszek. 1979. *Na drodze do kultury czynnej: o działalności instytutu Grotowskiego Teatr Laboratorium w latach 1970-1977* (On the Road to Active Culture: The Activities of Grotowski's Theatre Laboratory Institute in the Years 1970–77). Wrocław: Instytut Aktora—Teatr Laboratorium.

———. 1986. 'Poszukiwania etnologiczne współczesnej awangardy teatralnej' (Ethnological Research of the Contemporary Theatrical Avant-garde). PhD diss., University of Warsaw.

———. 2001. *Wielki mały wóz* (Big Small Vehicle). Gdańsk: Słowo/obraz terytoria.

———. 2009. 'Druga ojczyzna Grotowskiego: Haiti' (Grotowski's Second Homeland: Haiti). Talk given at the Year of Grotowski Inauguration, Wrocław, Poland, 14 January.

KRISTEVA, Julia. (1980). *Powers of Horror: An Essay on Abjection*. New York: Columbia University Press.

KUMIEGA, Jennifer. 1987. *The Theatre of Grotowski*. London: Methuen.

KUMIEGA, Jenna. 2001. 'Laboratory Theatre/Grotowski/The Mountain Project' in Richard Schechner and Lisa Wolford (eds), *The Grotowski Sourcebook*. London: Routledge, pp. 231–47.

LABORATORY THEATRE. n.d. *'Czuwanie' w Teatrze Laboratorium* ('The Vigil' in the Laboratory Theatre). Grotowski Institute Archive, Wrocław, Poland.

LAMBDIN, Thomas. 1990. 'The Gospel of Thomas' in James M. Robinson (ed.), *The Nag Hammadi Library*. Available at: http://gnosis.org/naghamm/gthlamb.html. (Last accessed on 12 March 2010).

MAGNAT, Virginie. 2005. 'Wykłady Grotowskiego w Collège de France' (Grotowski's lectures at the Collège de France) (Grzegorz Ziółkowski trans.). *Didaskalia Gazeta Teatralna* 67–8: 90–5.

MALRAUX, André. 1976. *La Métamorphose des Dieux*. Paris: Gallimard.

MEAD, George R. S. 1908. *Hymn of the Pearl—Acts of Thomas*. Available at: http://www.gnosis.org/library/hymnpearl.htm. (last accessed on 15 August 2015).

MENNEN Richard 1975. 'Jerzy Grotowski's paratheatrical projects'. *TDR* 19(4): 58–69

ORIZIO, Riccardo. 2000. *Lost White Tribes: Journeys among the Forgotten*. London: Secker & Warburg.

OSIŃSKI, Zbigniew. 1986. *Grotowski and His Laboratory*, 1st EDN. New York: PAJ Publications.

———. 1991. 'Grotowski Blazes the Trails: From Objective Drama to Ritual Arts' (Ann Herron and Halina Filipowicz trans.). *TDR* 35(1): 95–112.

———. 1998. *Grotowski: Źródła, inspiracje, konteksty* (Grotowski: Sources, Inspirations, Contexts). Gdańsk: Słowo/obraz terytoria.

———. 2001a. 'Grotowski Blazes the Trails: From Objective Drama to Art as vehicle' in Richard Schechner and Lisa Wolford (eds), *The Grotowski Sourcebook*. London: Routledge, pp. 385–400.

———. 2001b. *Ośrodki kulturowe w Polsce na przykładzie Ośrodka Badań Twórczości Jerzego Grotowskiego i Poszukiwań Teatralno-Kulturowych we Wrocławiu w latach 1990–2001* (Cultural Centres in Poland Based on the Example of the Centre of Study of Jerzy Grotowski's Work and for Cultural and Theatrical Research in Wrocław, 1990–2001). Available at: http:// www.grotowski-institute.art.pl/files/osrodki-kul-turowe-w-polsce.pdf. (last accessed on 4 June 2013).

———. 2008. 'Returning to the Subject: The Heritage of Reduta in Grotowski's Laboratory Theatre' (Kris Salata trans.). *TDR* 52(2): 52–74.

———. 2009. 'Grotowski and Kantor Lecture'. Tisch School of the Arts, New York University, 4 May.

PACHOŃSKI, Jan, and Reuel K. Wilson. 1986. *Poland's Caribbean Tragedy: A Study of Polish Legions in the Haitian War of Independence, 1802–1803*. Boulder: East European Monographs; New York: Columbia University Press.

PATTERSON, Stephen, James Robinson and Hans-Gebhard Bethge. 1998. *The Fifth Gospel*. Harrisburg, PA: Trinity Press International. Available at: http://gnosis.org/naghamm/gth_pat_rob.htm. (last accessed on 18 August 2015).

PERSZON, Jan. 1999. *Na brzegu życia i śmierci: Zwyczaje, obrzędy oraz wierzenia pogrzebowe i zaduszkowe na Kaszubach* (On the Brink of Life and Death: Customs, Rites and Beliefs of Kashubian Funerary and All Souls' Day Practices). Lublin: Towarzystwo Naukowe Katolickiego Uniwersytetu Lubelskiego.

PLOMIN, Robert, John C. DeFries, Ian W. Craig and Peter McGuffin. 2003. *Behavioral Genetics in the Postgenomic Era*. Washington, DC: American Psychological Association Press.

POLLASTRELLI, Carla. 2009. 'Grotowski: Theatre and Beyond.' Paper presented at the British Grotowski Conference, University of Kent. 11 June.

RENAN, Ernest. 1904. *Żywot Jezusa* (The Life of Jesus) (Andrzej Niemojewski trans.). Kraków: Drukarnia Narodowa.

RICHARDS, Thomas. 1995. *At Work with Grotowski on Physical Actions*. London: Routledge.

———. 2008. *Heart of Practice: Within the Workcenter of Jerzy Grotowski and Thomas Richards*. London: Routledge.

———. 2009. Interview with author, 26 August. Transcript.

———. 2010. 'At Work with Grotowski: The Early Years at Workcenter'. A Discussion with Thomas Richards and Mario Biagini. John Jay College of Criminal Justice, City University of New York, New York. 1 April.

ROBART, Maud. 2001. 'Między sztuką rytualną a sztuką teatru' (Between Ritual Arts and Theatre Arts). *Notatnik Teatralny* 50: 241–53.

———. 2009. Personal communication with author, 19 February.

RÓŻYCKI, Robert (ed.). 1992. 'Wyprawy terenowe "Teatru Źródeł"' (Fieldwork Conducted During the 'Theatre of Sources'). *Notatnik Teatralny* 4: 142–57.

RUTTER, Michael, and Judy Silberg. 2002. 'Gene-Environment Interplay in Relation to Emotional and Behavioral Disturbance'. *Annual Review of Psychology* 53: 463–90.

RYPSON, Sebastian. 2008. *Being Poloné in Haiti*. Warszawa: Oficyna Wydawnicza ASPRA-JR.

SCHECHNER, Richard, and Lisa Wolford (eds). 2001[1997]. *The Grotowski Sourcebook*. London: Routledge.

SCHECHNER, Richard. 2009. 'In a Dialogue About Grotowski'. Talk given at the Year of Grotowski Inauguration International Conference, Wrocław, Poland, 13 January.

SEYFERTH, Katharina. 2010. Phone interview with author, 19 February.

SHAWN, Wallace, and André Gregory. 1981. *'My Dinner With André': A Screenplay for the Film by Louis Malle*. New York: Grove Press.

SLOWIAK, James, and Jairo Cuesta. 2007. *Jerzy Grotowski*. London: Routledge.

TAVIANI, Ferdinando. 2009. 'Grotowski's Double Vision' in Paul Allain (ed.) *Grotowski's Empty Room*. London: Seagull Books, pp. 116–48.

THIBAUDAT, Jean-Pierre. 1995. 'Grotowski, un véhicule du théâtre' (Grotowski, A Vehicle of Theatre'). *Liberation*, 1 March, pp. 35–6.

THOMSON, Ian. 1992. *Bonjour Blanc! A Journey through Haiti*. London: Hutchinson Random House Group.

TURNER, John D. 1975. *The Book of Thomas*. The Nag Hammadi Library of the Gnostic Society Library. Available at: http://gnosis.org/naghamm/bookt-jdt-ln.html. (last accessed on 19 August 2015).

VOHRA, Ashok. 2003. 'Metaphysical Unity, Phenomenological Diversity and the Approach to the Other: Hindu Perspective on Xenophobia and the Hope for Human Flourishing' in Alon Goshen-Gottestein (ed.), *Religion Society and the Other: Hos-*

tility, Hospitality and the Hope of Human Flourishing. Jerusalem: The Elizah Interfaith Academy, pp. 93–108.

WETHAL, Torgeir. 1971. *Trening al teatro-laboratorio di Wrocław* (Training at the Laboratory Theatre). RAI. DVD.

WOLFORD, Lisa. 1991. 'Subjective Reflections on Objective Work: Grotowski in Irvine'. *TDR* 35(1): 165–80.

———. 1996. *Grotowski's Objective Drama Research.* Jackson: University Press of Mississippi.

———. 2001. 'General Introduction: Ariadne's Thread: Grotowski's Journey Through the Theatre' in Richard Schechner and Lisa Wolford (eds), *The Grotowski Sourcebook.* London: Routledge, pp. 1–22.

WOLFORD WYLAM, Lisa. 2008. 'Living Tradition: Continuity of Research at the Workcenter of Jerzy Grotowski and Thomas Richards.' *TDR* 52(2): 126–49.

YATES, Frances A. 1966. *The Art of Memory.* London: Routledge & Keegan Paul.

ZIÓŁKOWSKI, Grzegorz. 2001. 'Ośrodek, czyli jak złapać pstrąga' (The Centre; or, On How to Catch a Trout). *Didaskalia* 43–4 (July–August): 60–1.

ZÖCKLER, O. 1949–50. 'Vigils' in Lefferts Augustine Loetscher (ed.), *Schaff-Herzog Encyclopedia.* Grand Rapids, MI: Baker, p. 187.

INDEX

Page numbers in italics refer to images

Action (performative structure) 43, 44,
    53n20, 86, 87, 94, 95, 113
Action 53n20, 87, 88, 101–2, 104
Active Culture 59, 62, 77
Afro-Haitian songs 99, 115, 138, 140, 141
Ahrne, Marianne 30, 52n11, 52n13,
Akropolis 82–83, 87, 91n20, 91n22, 92n23
alchemy 97
aliveness 37, 38–9, 45. *See also* organicity
Amiar, Souphiène 109
ancestral memories 21–55
ancient mysteries 96–8
Art as vehicle 2, 15, 21, 31, 36, 37, 39, 41–5,
    48, 50n1, 53n14, 85, 86–7, 89, 93–117,
    138, 148
Artaud, Antonin 147
Association of Socialist Youth (Związek
    Młodzieży Socjalistycznej, ZMS) 10
associations 17, 21–2, 24, 28–30, 37, 42, 80,
    109, 118n11

Bacci, Roberto 93
Barba, Eugenio 17, 105
Beehives 62, 73, 90n9
Biagini, Mario 30, 35, 37, 38, 46, 101, 102,
    105–6
body of essence 46, 47, 50, 107, 119n20, 136
body-and-essence 46
body-being 44, 150
body-life 24, 25–6

body-memory 1, 5, 24–8, 36, 49
Brook, Peter 82–5, 87, 92n23, 92n24, 93, 96
Brunton, Paul 99
Brzezinka 56, 58, 61, 62, 66
Buber, Martin 114–5

Cadet, Eliezer 139, 144n13
Cadet, Micado 139, 144n13
Cazale 122, 124–5, 127–8, 144n14
Cieślak, Ryszard 26, 27, 28, 29, 28–30,
    52nn11–12, 57, 59, 60, 61, 62, 65, 77,
    79–80, 85, 86, 90n4, 105, 118n11,
    119n18, 133
Collège de France 50n2, 80, 91n21
Constant Prince, The 27, 28, 29, 28–30,
    52n12, 77, 79–80, 85, 86, 101, 119n18,
    133
Cuesta, Jairo 65, 79, 135, 138, 139

density of the body 96
Deren, Maya 50n2
doer 22, 37, 38–9, 40, 41–4, 45, 48, 50n1,
    53n15, 81, 86–8, 89, 94–5, 96, 104–5,
    106, 107–8, 109, 113, 114, 115, 116–7,
    137, 141–2, 150
Downstairs Action 43, 53n20
Eliade, Mircea 96–7
essence 1, 2, 4, 16, 27, 45–9, 50, 73–4, 77–8,
    81, 89, 111, 136, 137, 147, 148
Flaszen, Ludwik 11, 11–2, 34, 60, 83–4

Frémon, Amon 3, *125*, 125–32, 137, 139, 144n11, 145n18

Garoute, Jean-Claude 'Tiga' 32, 53n14, 124, 127, 139–40

gnosticism 97, 119–20n22

Gospel of Thomas 3, 101–2, 103–4

Gregory, André 65, 90n9

Gregory, Mercedes (Chiquita) 68

Grotowska, Emilia 6, 98, 101

Grotowski Centre 4

Grotowski Institute 4, 64, 91n13, 128

Grotowski, Feliks 122, 123, 124, 144n9

Grotowski, Kazimierz 6, 7, 34, 98

Gurdjieff, George Ivanovich 46, 47, 55n27, 82, 134, 135, 145n20

Haiti 3, 32, 35, 121, 122–4, 127, 128, 129, 130, 131, 132, 138, 139–40, 143n2, 143n4, 143n6, 143n8, 143n10

Holiday 62, 76–8

horizontality 95

Hymn of the Pearl 3, 109, 113, 116

I-I 46, 47, 106–7, 112, 114–6, 148

I-it 114, 115

I-Thou 114, 115

impulses 1, 17, 18, 21, 23, 24, 25–6, 30, 33, 43, 50n2, 81

induction 88, 89

inner action 40, 141, 142

intentions 1, 23, 60, 61, 64, 75, 109, 118n12

Jacob's ladder 93, 96

Janowski, Mieczysław 52n12

Jesus 76, 100, 101, 103, 104, 106, 118n12

Jimenez, Pablo 93

Journey to the East 62

Kantor, Tadeusz 89n2, 117

Kirshenblatt-Gimblett, Barbara 135–6

Kolankiewicz, Leszek 24, 75, 117n1, 123, 129, 144n13

Laboratory Theatre 19n6, 21, 34, 57, 59, 60, 62, 64, 65, 72, 80, 81, 82, 83, 84, 87, 88, 90n4, 90nn9–10, 91n20, 118n11, 144n10

Little Red Balloon 7, 13

luminescence 24

Luria, Isaac 72

Main Action 36–7, 54n20

Malraux, André 139

man of knowledge (*człowiek poznania*) 40, 95, 117n3, 148

Mars, Louis 138, 145n22

Meditations Aloud 60, 61

memory 1, 2, 5, 16, 18, 19nn5–6, 21–55, 111, 112, 149

memory-bridge 42

Meyerhold, Vsevolod 8

Molik, Zygmunt 60

montage 21, 23, 93–4, 96, 105

Mountain of Flame 61, 63, 65, 75, 91n18

Mountain Project 61, 62, 63, 65–6

movement and repose 103

Movements 134–5, 145n20

Nienadówka 6, 98, 99. See also *With Jerzy Grotowski, Nienadówka*

Night Vigil 2, 61, 62, 63, 64, 72, 75

Objective Drama 15, 53n14, 53n20, 94, 124; Objective Drama programme 19n2, 32, 35, 49, 86, 93, 117n2, 140, 141

objectivity 94, 95

Odin Teatret 118n11

organicity 17, 18, 36–7, 38, 39, 45, 46,
    50–1n2, 91n19, 96. *See also* aliveness

organon 32. *See also* yantra

Osiński, Zbigniew 7, 8, 18n1, 19nn2–3, 34,
    60, 73, 74, 90n6, 96, 97, 117n4, 117–
    18n9, 118n10, 123, 144nn8–9

Paluchiewicz, Andrzej 4, *9*, *11*, *15*, *20*, *28*,
    29, *56*, *58*, 60, *61*, 90n8

Paratheatre 15, 59, 78, 135, 138

physical actions 14, 16, 16–18, 38, 51n7

physical score 23, 28–9, 37

Polish legionnaires 121–3, 129, 143n3

Pollastrelli, Carla 26, 51n9, 93

Poloné-Ayisyen (Polish Haitians) 22

Pontedera 53n20, 86, 93, 140

pontifex 81–2

relationality 1, 3, 78, 107, 115, 116, 117, 132,
    137, 147, 149

Remembering Action 43–4, 54n20

remémoriser 30–1

reminiscence 31, 49–50

Renan, Ernest 99, 100, 101, 118n12

rhythm 25–6, 38, 68, 81, 99, 139

Richards, Thomas 4, 17, 18, 19n2, 22, 26,
    31, 35, 36–40, 41–9, 50n1, 51n7, 54n23,
    86, 87, 88, 93, 102, 104–6, 107, 108–9,
    113, 124, 131, 135, 138, 140, 141–2,
    147–8, 150

Road, The 63, 73

Robart, Maud 32, 35, 49, 53n14, 121, 124,
    127, 139, 140, 141

Saint-Soleil 32, 124, 127, 128, 138, 139

secular mysteries 97

self-discovery 44, 104, 107, 136, 148

self-penetration 1, 21, 23

self-realization 1, 148

Seyferth, Katharina 65–8, 71, 91n11

Slowiak, James 32, 79, 93

Special Project 60, 61, 62

Spiritual Canticle 29

Stanislavsky, Konstantin 8, 14, 16–8,
    19nn4–6, 24, 50–1n2, 51n7

stream of life 17, 81

tempo-rhythm 38, 99

testification 1, 2, 85, 86, 88, 148

Theatre of Nations 62, 90n10, 144n10

Theatre of Productions 1, 13, 15, 19n2, 21,
    32, 57, 59–60, 74, 77, 86–7, 91n19, 93,
    97, 118n11, 133

Theatre of Sources 15, 32, 95, 103, 117n5,
    123, 124, 127, 128, 135, 137, 138–9,
    145n21

Theatre of Thirteen Rows 11, 12

Thibaudat, Jean-Pierre 98, 106, 137–8

transformation of energy 39, 87

transgenerational memory 21, 32–6

transmission 1, 3, 4, 5, 21, 32, 35, 36, 49,
    54n24, 104–5, 109, 117, 121–46, 148–9

twin 1, 103–4, 105, 106, 112, 113, 116,
    119n19, 148, 149

twinship 3, 103, 104, 105, 106, 107, 109,
    115

Twin, The 3, 109, 112, 113, 119n21

Union of Polish Youth (Związek Młodzieży
    Polskiej, ZMP) 7

verticality 3, 4, 30, 92n25, 94–6, 99, 105,
    113, 149

Vigil, The 2, 57, 64–5, 66–7, 68, 70, 71, 72,
    73–5, 78, 79, 88, 91n11

vigilance 1, 2, 5, 57–92, 112–3, 114, 148, 149

Vodou 3, 23, 24, 124, 125, 127, 139–40, 143n5, 145n23. *See also* Frémon, Amon

Watching 79

With Jerzy Grotowski, Nienadówka 98, 100, 117n5, 144n14

witnessing 1, 2, 4, 5, 57–92, 148, 149; and martyrdom 85; and testification 1, 2, 88, 148

Wolford Wylam, Lisa (Lisa Wolford) 19n2, 33, 53n17, 94, 96, 98, 105–6, 112, 113, 117n2, 119n18, 119n21, 141

Workcenter of Jerzy Grotowski and Thomas Richards 4, 43, 51n9, 87, 93, 102–3, 105, 109, 118n13, 124, 138, 140, 150

yantra 32–3, 36. *See also* organon

yanvalou 2, 138

Zavadsky, Yuri 8

Zeami, Kanze (Zeami Motokiyo) 46, 54n26

Zmysłowski, Jacek 2, 57, 60, 62, 65–7, 68–9, 70, 71–2, 73–4, 78–9, 90n7